THE DEHYDRATOR COOKBOOK

Joanna White

BRISTOL PUBLISHING ENTERPRISES, INC.
San Leandro, California

A Nitty Gritty® Cookbook

Printed in the United States of America.

ISBN 1-55867-067-X

Cover design: Frank Paredes
Cover photography: John Benson
Food stylist: Suzanne Carreiro
Illustrator: James Balkovek
Back cover photography: Shel Izen

CONTENTS

DEHYDRATING FOODS
General Information

Welcome to the wonderful food preserving method of dehydrating! In the pages that follow, you will learn the advantages of this easy, economical approach to preserving produce and meats, and all of the techniques required. You will be introduced to some delicious recipes as well.

This book is divided into six sections: general information, including drying techniques; fruits; vegetables; meats; fish; and a section about other ways to utilize the dehydrator. The fruit and vegetable sections are in alphabetical order. These sections list preparation, pretreatment, dehydrating times and temperatures, rehydrating information and ways to utilize the dried produce. Recipes follow each fruit or vegetable to give you examples of ways to use the preserved food. Since most recipes call for rehydrated produce, you can actually substitute fresh foods as well.

This book is different from other dehydrating books because I have chosen to use lower dehydrating temperatures and only ascorbic acid (vitamin C) as the pretreatment solution, as opposed to sulfuring or sulfite solutions. When pretreatment without solutions is used, I recommend steam blanching instead of boiling. The purpose behind keeping the drying temperatures low (around 100°) and using steam blanching is to retain as many nutrients and digestive enzymes in the food as possible.

THE ADVANTAGES OF DEHYDRATING FOODS

- Dehydrating is inexpensive and the least time-consuming of all food preserving methods.

- Dried food takes up little storage space.

- There is no energy cost for storage (except for meat products).

- Drying is easy to do. Results are nutritious to eat and versatile to utilize.

- Dehydrating is a great way to use excessive produce during peak seasons.

- Preserve leftovers — stews, sauces, bean dishes, etc. can be dried to use at a later date.

- Dehydrated foods are excellent for backpacking, camping, fishing, skiing, or any outdoor sport. Dried foods keep well without refrigeration and are low in bulk and weight.

- If you have children, one of the best reasons to own a dehydrator is to make fruit leathers. Leathers are probably the most popular of dried foods and make great "all natural" candy-like snacks.

NUTRITIONAL VALUES OF DRIED FOODS

- Dried food is about equal to frozen food in nutritional value.

- Drying is superior to canning because the high temperatures needed to process canned foods can destroy as much as 65 percent of the original food value (especially vitamin C, thiamine and riboflavin).

- There is some loss of vitamin A and C during the drying process, but the majority of loss is during the blanching step before drying. I prefer to steam treat for less vitamin loss.
- Since dried foods reduce down to about ¼ the original weight, they are really concentrated nutritional powerhouses.

PREPARING FOODS FOR DRYING

1. All produce should be perfect for drying. Blemished or bruised fruit will not keep as well and may spoil the whole batch.
2. Fruit should be fully ripe so that the sugar content is at its peak.
3. Wash all produce well to remove dirt, insect larvae and bacteria. Trim away any bruised or soft spots.
4. Cut the fruits or vegetables to a consistent size so that they will dry at the same rate.
5. The larger the piece of food, the longer it will take to dry, so keep pieces small.
6. Remove the pits, stems, stones and peelings if desired. Halve and/or slice into uniform pieces and then pretreat if desired. I've listed the best methods of pretreatment under each of the individual fruits or vegetables.

NOTE: Any waxed peelings should definitely be removed before drying. Otherwise, the decision to peel or not to peel has mixed reviews. Peelings have more vitamins, but the peeling causes the produce to take longer to dry, which in turn causes vitamin loss and sometimes a slightly bitter taste. You'll have to make your own decision on this matter.

PRETREATMENT METHODS FOR DRIED FOODS

Natural: Slice fruit directly into either lemon or pineapple juice. Allow the fruit to sit in the undiluted juice for approximately 2 minutes before draining and place on the drying trays.

Ascorbic Acid: Otherwise known as powdered vitamin C, use 3 tablespoons per quart of water. Slice the fruit into the solution for 2 minutes, drain and place on trays to dry.

Sodium Bisulfite: With public warnings against sulfites and because so many people have allergic reactions to sulfites, I am not recommending this method. But for those who wish to use sodium bisulfite, use food safe (USP) grade only. Dissolve 1 tsp. of sodium bisulfite in 1 quart of water. Dip produce in the solution for 2 minutes, drain and place on trays to dry.

Steam Blanching: Place the vegetables in a steamer basket, add water to the pot, being careful not to allow the water to touch the food, cover with a lid and steam for the recommended time. Immediately chill the vegetables in cold running water and drain thoroughly. This is the preferred method of pretreatment for vegetables since it keeps the internal temperature of the vegetable low, thus retaining more vitamins and digestive enzymes.

Water Blanching: Place the prepared produce in boiling water and measure the time when the water resumes boiling. Boil for the recommended time, chill by running the produce under cold water, drain and place on the trays to dry.

Syrup Blanching: Combine 1 cup sugar, 1 cup corn syrup, 2 cups water and 1 tsp. ascorbic acid powder together in a heavy saucepan. Bring the ingredients to a boil and add the sliced, prepared fruit. Simmer for about 5 to 10 minutes, depending on the variety and thickness of the fruit. This makes a very sweet dried fruit and takes longer to dehydrate. If you reuse the syrup, add more water as the solution evaporates with boiling.

Sulfuring: Must be done outdoors because the sulfur dioxide fumes can be harmful to your lungs and irritating to the mucous membranes. The fruits are arranged on wooden trays that are stacked and under cover. Approximately 1 tablespoon of sulfur dioxide is used per pound of fresh fruit. The sulfur is burned in a dish under the trays for approximately 4 hours (times differ according to the specific fruit). The fruit is then dehydrated outdoors, again to protect you against the fumes. I do not recommend this method for the same reason I do not like to use the sulfiting solutions.

Checking: Because some fruits have a natural protective coating like figs, grapes, blueberries, plums, etc., they need to be dipped in boiling water to cause the skins to burst slightly, which will allow moisture to escape. The fruit is dipped for approximately 2 minutes and then placed on the trays to dry. This helps the fruit dry considerably faster, which reduces the nutritional loss.

DRYING METHODS

Electric Dehydrator: The most popular method used which involves electric heat and circulating air. It produces the best quality of dried product without the problems of bad weather, unsanitary conditions or constant watching. All the times for dehydrating in this book are based on using an electric dehydrator. I've chosen to use the lowest temperature setting whenever possible to reduce the vitamin loss and avoid destroying the digestive enzymes in the food.

Sun Drying: A wonderful method if the conditions are perfect. You need consecutive sunny days (ideally in the 90s), low humidity, low air pollution and good air circulation. Sun drying takes considerably longer than using electric dehydrators and has a danger of the food being infested by insects. The food is placed on nonmetal trays, covered with a protective netting like a cheesecloth and placed in direct sunlight where there is good air circulation. The food must be checked frequently and rotated. Produce with higher sugar contents are better for sun drying. The fruits and vegetables recommended for sun drying are: apples, apricots, cherries, chili peppers, citrus peels, coconut, currants, dates, figs, grapes, lentils, nectarines, peaches, pears, peas, pineapples, plums, shell beans and soybeans.

Oven Drying: Can be used for drying small amounts of food in a hurry, but the cost of heating an oven far exceeds the costs of using an electric dehydrator. The oven must be propped open to keep the temperature low since most ovens rarely go below 200°. The food must be rotated frequently and there are problems with some produce not drying properly because the skin may prevent moisture loss in the center which leads to eventual spoilage. Microwaves are not good for dehydrating because they have a tendency to cook the food instead of drying it.

Homemade Dryers: There are many plans available to build your own dehydrator. It is important to have a fan to rotate the air and a good consistent temperature. The heating source should be on the back or on the side of the dryer so the bottom tray does not scorch easily.

Solar Dryers: Solar dryers collect the sun's rays and elevate the temperature. As with the sun dryers, solar dryers are subject to weather changes and need frequent rotating. If you chose this method, try to find a dryer with a fan to lessen drying time.

Stove-Top Dryers: This is an old technique used during pioneer days with the aid of a wood-burning stove. Generally, the trays sit on top of the stove and the temperature needs to be monitored closely. The advantage is that it is usually done indoors, thus less insect infestation, but the stove is not available for regular use during the drying process.

STORING DRIED FOODS

1. Check food for dryness. Pieces not uniform in size have a tendency to dry at different rates. Remove from the dehydrator only the pieces that are dry and leave the others for a longer period.
2. Pasteurization: If you suspect that there might be some infestation from insects, freeze the packaged dried food for at least 48 hours before placing into storage containers.

3. Once you are sure the food is completely dry and free from infestation, store the dried foods in glass jars, plastic containers or food grade heavy plastic freezer bags which are stored in metal or plastic containers with tight-fitting lids.
4. Label each package of dried food with the contents, date and (if desired) include the rehydrating procedure.
5. Store the packaged dried food in a dry, dark, cool area. The lower the temperature, the longer the shelf life. Ideally dried foods should be kept below 60°. I do store my dried meat products in the freezer for extra protection.
6. If the food has been dried properly, it should last from 6 months to 1 year. If it is stored at low temperatures the shelf life can even be longer. Be careful to rotate your dried food to insure freshness and better nutritional value.
7. Periodically check your stored foods for mold, moisture or insects. If there is mold, throw the food out.

REHYDRATING DRIED FOODS

FRUIT: There are three methods of rehydrating fruit.

- Place the fruit in a steamer over boiling water and steam until fruit has plumped.

- Cover the dried fruit with water or fruit juice and let stand until fruit has plumped; drain.

- Cover the dried fruit with boiling water or heated fruit juice and let stand for approximately 10 minutes or until plump; then drain.

NOTE: Do not add sugar during the rehydrating process. It causes the fruit to absorb less water than it normally would.

VEGETABLES

- Vegetables rehydrate slower than fruits because they have lost more water.

- Vegetables are better if they are allowed to soak long enough to reabsorb most of their water before using for cooking.

- Dried vegetables can be used directly in heated liquid like soups, stews or sauces, but the vegetables will be tougher. It is best to rehydrate the vegetables first.

- Use just enough water or broth to cover the vegetables. Even though the quantity of liquid may vary depending on the type of vegetable used, the standard measure is: for every 1 cup of dried vegetables, use 1½ cups of liquid to rehydrate. Be sure to use the soaking water in your cooking because the water contains some of the nutrients.

- Rehydrating times vary according to the type of vegetable. The important thing to remember is not to leave the vegetables in the soaking water for more than 2 hours without refrigeration due to the danger of bacterial growth.

NOTE: Do not add salt to the rehydrating vegetables because it may inhibit water absorption.

COOKING DRIED FOODS

FRUIT

- Pour boiling water over the dried fruit, just to cover. Simmer, covered, for approximately 10 to 15 minutes. Remove from the heat and sweeten to taste, if desired.

- If the reconstituted fruit is to be used in a cooked dish, pour boiling water over the dried fruit, cover, and let it soak for several hours (or until tender).

- Try to use the soaking liquid in the recipes for the residual nutrients.

VEGETABLES

- For the best nutrition, with the exception of greens, soak all vegetables in cold water (just to cover) until close to the original texture before using them in cooking.

- Cook vegetables in the liquid that was used to rehydrate them.

- Greens should be covered with boiling water (just to cover) and simmered until tender.

- Vegetables can also be steamed to rehydrate, which would definitely speed up the rehydrating process.

- Dried vegetables can be added to hot dishes without rehydrating. Use 1 cup extra water for every cup of dried vegetables when adding to stew. Use 2 cups extra water for every cup of dried vegetables when adding to soup.

- When substituting dried food for fresh in recipes, 1 part dried vegetable equals about 3 cups fresh.

APPLES

PREPARATION: Wash, peel (if desired), core and slice into ¼-inch slices or rounds. Peels contain more nutrients but have a tendency to make fruit tougher to eat and longer to dry.

PRETREATMENT: Apples will definitely darken without pretreatment. Soak in ascorbic acid bath for 2 to 3 minutes before drying.

NOTE: For snack food, after pretreatment sprinkle with cinnamon sugar.

DEHYDRATE: Dry approximately 6 to 8 hours at 100° or until slightly crisp.

REHYDRATE: Cover with hot water and let soak about 10 to 15 minutes.

LEATHERS: Makes excellent leather. Simply puree fruit, add spices (if desired) and spread onto solid plastic sheet or plastic wrap. Dry approximately 16 to 18 hours at 100°.

NOTE: Because apples are naturally sweet, mix apple puree with more tart fruits until desired sweetness is attained.

SPECIAL NOTE: If you have apple trees and plan to do a lot of dehyrating, I would highly recommend that you purchase an automatic apple peeler. These peelers will peel, core and slice an apple in seconds, saving a tremendous amount of time and effort.

APPLE KUCHEN

This is a wonderful yeasted apple cake for breakfast or brunch.

¾ cup warm water
1 tbs. yeast
⅓ cup sugar
2¾ cups flour
2 tbs. nonfat dry milk
1 tsp. salt
3 tbs. butter
2 eggs
½ cup whipping cream

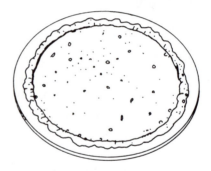

TOPPING
½ cup sugar
1½ cups rehydrated apples
⅓ cup cinnamon sugar (⅓ cup sugar and ½ tsp. cinnamon)

Dissolve yeast in warm water; add ⅓ cup sugar and about ½ cup flour to make a sponge. Place on a warm oven door to rise about 30 minutes. Mix remaining flour, dry milk and salt together in a food processor and process with butter about 10 seconds. Add risen yeast mixture and 1 egg and process about 40 seconds. (Note: If dough gets too sticky, turn machine off and let it rest about 2 minutes, and then finish processing). Roll dough out into a circle to fit a 9-inch pan, pressing dough up sides. Sprinkle with ¼ cup topping sugar over dough and place rehydrated apple slices on top. Beat whipping cream with remaining ¼ cup sugar and 1 egg together and pour over apples. Sprinkle top with cinnamon sugar. Bake in a 350° oven for 30 minutes or until a knife inserted comes out clean. Cool on a rack.

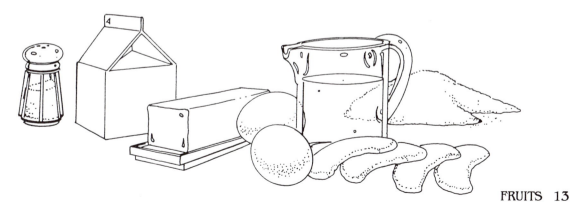

APPLE PIE

When apples are in season, consider drying them, especially the varieties that are good for baking — like Golden Delicious and pippins.

4½ cups boiling water
4 cups dried apples
½ to 1 cup sugar (depending on
   tartness of apple)
1 tsp. cinnamon

1 tbs. dried lemon peeling
2 tbs. tapioca
1 tbs. butter
one 9-inch double pie crust

Pour boiling water over dried apples and let set for about 30 minutes. Drain and reserve liquid for sauce. In a saucepan, combine apple liquid, sugar, cinnamon and lemon peeling, and heat to boiling. Add tapioca and boil for 1 minute. Remove mixture from heat and add butter, stirring until butter melts. Add rehydrated apples and let mixture cool before pouring into unbaked pie crust. Bake at 375° for approximately 40 minutes or until crust is golden brown.

APPLE SOUR CREAM CAKE

I think cakes are a great way to use dehydrated fruits because the aesthetics of dried fruit is not important. The sour cream makes this wonderfully moist.

3 cups flour
1 cup sugar
4 tsp. baking powder
1 tsp. salt
1 tsp. cinnamon
1 cup milk

½ cup softened butter
4 eggs, separated
2 cups rehydrated apples
1 cup sour cream
1 cup chopped walnuts
½ cup sugar

Mix together flour, 1 cup sugar, baking powder, salt, and cinnamon and set aside. Mix milk, butter, and 2 eggs together, add dry ingredients and blend until smooth. Stir in rehydrated apples and pour into a greased 9x13-inch baking pan. Blend sour cream with remaining 2 eggs and spread over batter. Mix walnuts and sugar together and sprinkle over batter. Bake at 375° for 35 to 45 minutes or until a knife inserted in the center comes out clean.

APPLE COCONUT COFFEE CAKE

Servings: 12

I liked this best served warm, right out of the oven for breakfast or brunch.

¾ cup butter
1 cup sugar
3 eggs
1½ cups flour
2 tsp. baking powder
¼ tsp. salt

½ cup milk
1 cup shredded coconut
1¼ cups rehydrated chopped apples
⅓ cup sliced almonds
3 tbs. sugar

Cream butter and 1 cup sugar together. Blend in eggs and beat well. Mix flour with baking powder and salt; add to creamed mixture alternately with milk, blending until smooth. Stir in coconut and apples. Pour into a well-greased 9-x-13-inch pan and sprinkle with almonds and 3 tbs. sugar. Bake in a 350° oven for 30 minutes or until a knife inserted comes out clean.

APPLE AND SAUSAGE SAUTÉ

A quick and simple dish for breakfast or brunch that comes from the maple syrup state, Vermont. To make it traditional, serve with baked beans and brown bread or baking powder biscuits.

1 lb. pork sausage (links or patties)
3 cups rehydrated apple rings
1 cup "pure" maple syrup
½ cup white or cider vinegar

Fry sausage until golden brown, drain, place on a cookie sheet and keep warm in a 200° oven. While sausage is browning, mix maple syrup and vinegar together over medium heat; reduce to simmer. Add rehydrated apple rings and simmer uncovered until apples are tender-crisp (about 5 minutes). Arrange apple rings on a platter with sausage, pour syrup mixture over all and serve immediately.

POACHED APPLES WITH CREME ANGLAISE

This is an incredibly delicious and creamy dessert. The sauces and poached apples can be cooked in advance and mixed together just before serving.

3 cups dried apple slices
½ cup dried grapes or currants
2 to 3 cups apple juice

Place dried apples and grapes in a saucepan with 2 cups apple juice. Bring mixture to a boil, turn heat to low and simmer, covered, until apples are tender-crisp. Add additional apple juice if mixture becomes dry. Drain off excess juice and cool.

CREME ANGLAISE

1¾ cups milk
6 egg yolks
½ cup sugar

¼ cup cream
1 tsp. vanilla

Scald milk and set aside. Place egg yolks and sugar in a bowl and beat until eggs turn pale yellow in color. Add hot milk and beat until smooth. Pour into a heavy saucepan and cook slowly over medium low heat until mixture thickens and coats back of a wooden spoon. Remove from heat and add cream and vanilla. Strain mixture through a sieve and cool. Cover mixture with waxed paper or plastic wrap and refrigerate until ready to use.

CARAMEL SAUCE

½ cup butter
½ cup white sugar

½ cup brown sugar
½ cup evaporated milk

Melt butter in a saucepan; add sugars and milk. Stir over medium heat until sauce thickens. Remove from heat until ready to use.

To serve: Place apples in bowl, pour on creme anglaise and drizzle with caramel sauce.

NOTE: To make this even more decadent, sprinkle with chopped, toasted macadamia nuts.

APRICOTS

PREPARATION: Wash, halve, remove pits and place on trays, cut-side down.
PRETREATMENT: Not a noticeable difference if treated with ascorbic acid bath, so I prefer not to treat.
NOTE: An alternative for better color and flavor if planning to rehydrate instead of using in its dried state is to syrup blanch before drying.
DEHYDRATE: Dry approximately 60 hours at 100°, or until pliable with no pockets of moisture.
REHYDRATE: Cover with hot water and let soak 15 minutes (unless apricots are cooked or used in sauces, dried apricots are usually better for baking if not rehydrated ahead of time).
LEATHERS: Excellent for leathers. Puree, taste and add a little corn syrup or honey, or mix with sweeter fruit puree if apricot puree is too sour. Dry approximately 16 to 18 hours at 100°.
SPECIAL NOTE: Dried apricots are probably the most common of dried fruits to use in cooking. Snipping with a scissors is the best method for cutting dried apricots.

APRICOT BREAD PUDDING

Servings: 8

Egg bread gives bread pudding a better flavor and a rich color.

1 lb. loaf egg bread
3 cups milk
1 cup cream
3 eggs
1½ cups sugar
1 to 2 tbs. almond extract
¾ cup chopped dried apricots
¾ cup dried green grapes or golden raisins
¾ cup slivered almonds
1 cup powdered sugar
½ cup butter
1 egg
¼ cup amaretto liqueur or to taste

Preheat oven to 350°. Cut or tear egg bread into pieces and place on a cookie sheet. Toast bread pieces in oven for about 15 minutes. Meanwhile mix 3 cups milk, cream, eggs and sugar together. Pour mixture over toasted bread pieces and let it absorb for 15 minutes. Add almond extract (to personal taste), apricots, dried grapes or raisins and almonds. Pour into a buttered casserole dish. Place casserole dish inside another baking dish and put in oven. Pour boiling water into outside dish. (This is known as a bain marie and is the best method for cooking custard-type desserts.) Bake for 1 hour. In a saucepan, mix powdered sugar, butter and egg and bring just to a boil. Remove from heat and add amaretto. Serve over warm bread pudding.

APRICOT SAUCE

This is a great sauce to serve over waffles, pancakes, or even over desserts like bread pudding.

1 cup rehydrated apricots
½ cup maple syrup
2 tbs. cornstarch
1 cup apricot nectar
1 tbs. lemon juice
3 tbs. honey
pinch of cinnamon

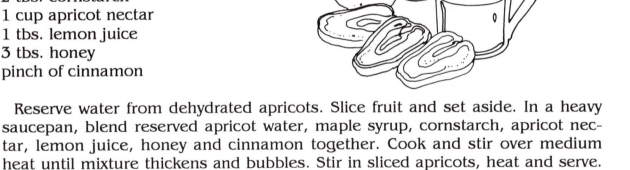

Reserve water from dehydrated apricots. Slice fruit and set aside. In a heavy saucepan, blend reserved apricot water, maple syrup, cornstarch, apricot nectar, lemon juice, honey and cinnamon together. Cook and stir over medium heat until mixture thickens and bubbles. Stir in sliced apricots, heat and serve.

APRICOT ZUCCHINI BREAD

Makes: 2 loaves

A great recipe utilizing both dehydrated apricots and zucchini. Try rehydrating some extra apricots and mixing with cream cheese and a little powdered sugar to serve as a spread on this bread.

1 cup oil
2 cups sugar
1 tbs. vanilla
3 eggs
2 cups rehydrated grated zucchini
1 lb. rehydrated apricots (drained well)

3 cups flour
2 tsp. baking soda
1 tsp. baking powder
1 tsp. salt
2 tsp. nutmeg
1 cup chopped walnuts

Preheat oven to 350°. Line 2 loaf pans with greased brown paper and grease sides of pans. Beat together oil, sugar and vanilla. Add eggs, one at a time, beating well. Add well-drained zucchini and finely chopped apricots and beat well. Sift flour, baking soda, baking powder, salt and nutmeg together. Stir into creamed mixture. Add chopped nuts. Pour batter into prepared pans and bake for approximately 50 minutes or until a knife inserted into center comes out clean. Cool 10 minutes before removing bread from pans.

BANANAS

PREPARATION: Avoid over-ripe bananas. Simply peel and slice into even pieces.

PRETREATMENT: Soak in a ascorbic acid bath 2 to 3 minutes before drying.

DEHYDRATE: Dry approximately 55 hours at 100° or until crisp.

REHYDRATE: Cover with hot water for about 10 minutes and drain. Approximately 1 cup tightly packed dry bananas will rehydrate to 2 cups.

LEATHER: Puree fruit, add a little ascorbic acid to prevent discoloration and pour onto trays. Dry approximately 18 hours at 100° or until pliable.
NOTE: Because bananas are so sweet, use them to add to less sweet fruit purees.

SPECIAL NOTE: Dried bananas are great as a snack or used in trail mixes or cereals. Rehydrated bananas are good for bakery products like breads, cakes and cookies.

BEST EVER BANANA BREAD

Makes: 2 loaves

This is my favorite banana bread recipe — what else can I say!

2 cups sugar
1 cup butter
3 cups rehydrated bananas
4 eggs
1 tsp. banana extract
2½ cups cake flour
2 tsp. baking soda
1 tsp. salt

Preheat oven to 350°. Line 2 loaf pans with greased brown paper and grease sides of pans. With a mixer, cream sugar and butter until light and fluffy. Mash bananas and add to creamed mixture along with eggs and banana extract; beat well. Sift cake flour, soda and salt together and blend with banana mixture (do not overmix). Pour into prepared pans and bake for approximately 50 minutes or until a knife inserted in center comes out clean. Cool for 10 minutes before removing from pans.

WHOLE WHEAT BANANA NUT BREAD

Makes: 2 loaves

Here's a whole wheat bread loaded with flavor that kids always go for.

1 cup melted butter
2 cups sugar
4 beaten eggs
1 tsp. banana extract
2 cups rehydrated bananas
2 cups white flour

1 tsp. salt
2 tsp. soda
2 cups whole wheat flour
⅔ cup hot water
1 cup chopped walnuts

Preheat oven to 325°. Line 2 loaf pans with greased brown paper and grease sides of pans. With a mixer, beat butter and sugar together. Add eggs, banana extract and mashed rehydrated bananas, and blend until smooth. Sift white flour with salt and soda; stir in whole wheat flour. Add dry ingredients to banana mixture alternately with hot water. Stir in nuts. Pour batter into loaf pans and bake 1 hour or until a knife inserted into center of loaf comes out clean. Cool 10 minutes before removing from pans.

BERRIES

blackberries, boysenberries, huckleberries, loganberries, marion berries, and raspberries

PREPARATION: Simply remove any stems, wash and shake dry before placing on trays. You may need to use a netted tray if berries are small so they won't fall through the normal tray holes.

PRETREATMENT: None is necessary.

DEHYDRATE: Dry approximately 100 hours at 100° or until brittle (drying time will vary according to size of berry).

REHYDRATE: Pour hot water over berries and let soak about 15 minutes. Drain well before using.

LEATHERS: Berries make excellent fruit leathers. Puree berries, strain to remove seeds, taste and adjust sweetness to your personal preference using corn syrup, honey or other sweet fruit purees. Dehydrate approximately 16 to 18 hours at 100° or until pliable.

SPECIAL NOTES: Other than fruit leathers, berries are not as desirable as other dried fruit (in their dried form) because of the seeds. If you rehydrate the berries, always consider straining seeds before using in recipes.

BERRY ICE

Berries are best used in fruit leathers. But another possibility is utilizing them in recipes where you rehydrate, puree and strain out the seeds before using. Try blackberries, boysenberries, marion berries, raspberries or any combination of these berries.

4 cups rehydrated berries
1 cup sugar (or to taste)
1 tbs. lemon juice
½ cup water

In a blender or food processor, whirl rehydrated berries until pureed. Strain out seeds with a sieve. Mix strained puree with sugar, lemon juice and water. Freeze in a shallow dish until almost hard; whirl again (to incorporate some air, which lightens mixture). Return to freezer and freeze well. Serve garnished with mint leaves.

BLUEBERRIES

PREPARATION: Remove stems, wash berries and drain.

PRETREATMENT: Dip in boiling water for 1 to 2 minutes or until skins are cracked.

DEHYDRATE: Dry approximately 10 hours at 100° or until leathery.

REHYDRATE: Cover with hot water and soak for 15 minutes.

LEATHERS: Best if combined with other fruit. Dry approximately 16 to 18 hours at 100°.

SPECIAL NOTES: Blueberries lose some of their aesthetic value with dehydrating but work well in recipes such as muffins or breads.

BLUEBERRY MUFFINS

Everyone loves blueberry muffins. Blueberries are the ideal diet food because they are low in sugar and help regulate the body's insulin production.

3 cups flour
4 tsp. baking powder
½ tsp. salt
1 cup sugar
½ tsp. mace (or nutmeg)
2 tbs. dried lemon peel

2 cups rehydrated blueberries (or
  1 cup dried)
2 eggs
4 tbs. melted butter
1 cup milk

Preheat oven to 400°. Grease or paper-line muffin tins. Mix flour, baking powder, salt, sugar, mace and lemon peel together and gently fold in blueberries. (Note: iI using rehydrated blueberries, make sure they are dry before adding to flour mixture). Beat eggs; add melted butter and milk. Add egg mixture to flour mixture and fold until just barely mixed. Spoon into muffin tins and bake 20 to 25 minutes. If desired, spread top of muffin with warmed honey when you first remove muffins from oven to give it a little more eye appeal and slight sweetness.

BLUEBERRY APPLE COBBLER

Every once in awhile I like good old-fashioned cooking and this fits the craving. I've used both dehydrated blueberries and apples but, of course, fresh can be used for either fruit.

2 cups rehydrated blueberries
1 cup rehydrated sliced apples
2 tbs. dark brown sugar
1 cup flour
3/4 cup sugar
1 tsp. baking powder

3/4 tsp. salt
1 beaten egg
1/3 cup melted butter
3 tbs. sugar
3/4 tsp. cinnamon

Preheat oven to 375°. Butter a 9-x-13-inch pan. Drain blueberries and apples well, mix with brown sugar and evenly distribute coated fruits on bottom of pan. Mix flour, sugar, baking powder and salt together and stir in beaten egg. Cover fruits with mixture and pour melted butter on top of batter. Mix 3 tbs. sugar and cinnamon together and sprinkle over top. Bake for 30 minutes or until top is firm to the touch and browned.

CANTALOUPE

PREPARATION: Peel, seed and cut into ¼-inch thick pieces.

PRETREATMENT: No pretreatment is necessary.

DEHYDRATE: Dry approximately 33 hours at 100° or until pliable.

REHYDRATE: Cover with cold water and soak about 2 hours.

LEATHERS: Puree and pour onto trays. Dry approximately 16 to 18 hours at 100°. Taste before drying to determine if you want to add sweeteners or mix with other fruit purees.

SPECIAL NOTE: Cantaloupe is not a common dried fruit product. I found that it will work with trail mix, but it is best if eaten in its dried state like candy.

FRUIT TRAIL MIX

Makes: 3 cups

Everyone likes trail mix. Don't limit yourself to this combination of fruit. Try at least one different fruit each time — the variations can be endless.

½ cup dried cantaloupe
½ cup dried banana chips
½ cup shredded coconut
½ cup mixed dried grapes (raisins)
⅓ cup chopped dried dates
¼ cup dried apricots, peaches or pears
1 cup mixed nuts, optional

Simply cut all fruit into small pieces and toss together. Add any combination of nuts, if desired. Store in an airtight container.

CHERRIES

PREPARATION: Wash, remove stems and pit.

PRETREATMENT: Drop in boiling water for 1 to 2 minutes to break skins.

DEHYDRATE: Depending on the size of the cherry, dry approximately 48 to 52 hours at 100° or until pliable with no pockets of moisture.

REHYDRATE: Pour hot water on top and soak for 15 to 20 minutes.

LEATHERS: Makes excellent leather. Dry 16 to 18 hours at 100°.

SPECIAL NOTES: Cherries are excellent snack foods. Aesthetically they look good after rehydrating and can be used in pies or used as a substitute for raisins in recipes.

CHERRY CREAM CHEESE SPREAD

Servings: 12

I think cherries are liked universally. This is a quick, simple appetizer spread using cherries flavored with liqueur.

1 cup rehydrated cherries (dark varieties)
½ cup amaretto or Grand Marnier liqueur
16 oz. cream cheese
1 tbs. sugar (or more taste)
1 cup toasted chopped almonds

Cover rehydrated cherries with liqueur and refrigerate for 24 hours. Drain. Beat cream cheese until fluffy; add sugar and cherries. Taste and adjust sweetness to your personal taste. Chill mixture and form into a ball. Cover ball with almonds (or mix into cream cheese mixture). Serve with plain crackers.

NOTE: If you prefer nonalcoholic, simply eliminate the liqueur-soaking step and add a little cherry, almond, or orange extract to the cream cheese mixture to your personal taste.

CITRUS FRUITS AND PEELS

grapefruit, lemons, limes and oranges

PREPARATION: Generally the fruits are dried with the peeling on (cut into thin, even slices). If only drying the peel, use a potato peeler or zester to remove the colored part of the peel (do not include the white pithy part).

PRETREATMENT: Not necessary.

DEHYDRATE: The fruits will require approximately 45 to 55 hours at 100° or until brittle. The peels require about 10 hours at 100° (depending on the size of the pieces) or until crisp.

REHYDRATE: Soak the fruits in cold water for about 2 hours or grind into a powder for spicing. The peels are usually not rehydrated, but ground into a powder and used as a spice.

LEATHERS: Because of the juiciness of the fruit, generally only a small amount of citrus fruits are added to other fruit purees. The natural acid helps prevent discoloring. The peels are added to fruit purees for additional flavor.

SPECIAL NOTES: It is difficult to dry sliced citrus fruits because their dryness deceives you. Make sure the fruit is very, very dry before storing; otherwise mold will result. I generally use dried citrus fruits to flavor water or punches.

CITRUS CREAM CHEESE FILLING

Makes: 2 cups

Cream cheese fillings can be used to fill fruit leathers, spread on tea breads or even as a spread for muffins or croissants.

8 oz. softened cream cheese
1 tbs. dried powdered citrus fruits
¼ cup sweetener (honey, fruit juice concentrate or sugar)
1 cup dried grapes (raisins) or chopped nuts

Simply mix all ingredients together. Taste and adjust sweetener to your personal preference.

FRUITS 37

CRANBERRIES

PREPARATION: Wash and drain.

PRETREATMENT: Drop cranberries into boiling water for 1 to 2 minutes or until skins crack.

DEHYDRATE: Dry approximately 12 hours at 100° or until leathery like a raisin.

REHYDRATE: Pour hot water on top and soak 15 minutes.

LEATHER: Cranberries are best combined with other fruits in fruit leathers. Dry approximately 16 to 18 hours at 100°.

NOTE: I tried drying canned cranberry sauce and found that it never dried sufficiently to be easily removed from the trays.

SPECIAL NOTE: Cranberries can be used like blueberries, either dried or rehydrated before adding to baking recipes.

CRANBERRY BREAD

When cranberries are plentiful, dry a large quantity so that you can enjoy them year-round.

¾ cup orange juice
1 cup dried cranberries
1 cup whole wheat flour
1 cup flour
½ cup wheat germ
¼ tsp. salt
2 tsp. baking powder

½ tsp. baking soda
¾ cup chopped nuts
1 tbs. dried orange rind
¾ cup honey
1 egg
2 tbs. oil

Preheat oven to 350°. Line a loaf pan with greased brown paper and grease sides of pan. Heat orange juice and add dried cranberries. Allow berries to sit for at least 15 minutes. Meanwhile combine flours, wheat germ, salt, baking powder, baking soda and nuts. Mix together orange rind, honey, egg, oil, orange juice and cranberries; add to dry mixture. Stir until just moistened. Spread into prepared loaf pan and bake 50 minutes or until a knife inserted in center comes out clean. Cool for 15 minutes, remove from pan and transfer to a rack. Cool completely before slicing.

CRANBERRY APPLE RELISH

Makes: 10 cups

Live a little! Try making your own relish instead of using canned for your next holiday event.

8 cups apples, peeled and sliced
3 cups rehydrated cranberries
2 cups sugar
1 cup boiling water
¼ cup cornstarch

Cook apples, cranberries and 1 cup sugar in boiling water over medium heat, stirring occasionally to be sure fruit does not stick to bottom of pan (approximately 5 to 7 minutes). Mix remaining 1 cup sugar and cornstarch together thoroughly before adding to fruit. Continue to cook and stir until sugar is dissolved and juice is clear. Cool and refrigerate until ready to serve.

CRANBERRY CHUTNEY

Makes: 6 cups

I love to serve cranberry chutney during the holidays. This is also great on turkey sandwiches with a little cream cheese and alfalfa sprouts.

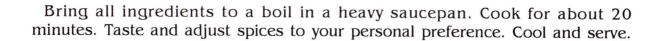

4 cups rehydrated cranberries
1 cup water
1 cup dehydrated grapes (raisins -mixing varieties is best)
2 cups sugar
1 large can crushed pineapple (drained)
1 tsp. dried ginger
1 tsp. dried cinnamon
½ tsp. dried allspice
½ tsp. salt

Bring all ingredients to a boil in a heavy saucepan. Cook for about 20 minutes. Taste and adjust spices to your personal preference. Cool and serve.

DATES

PREPARATION: Simply wash well, remove pits and cut in half.

PRETREATMENT: Not necessary.

DEHYDRATE: Most dates in the grocery store are already sun-dried. If you can get fresh dates, the drying time varies with the type of date. Dry approximately 15 to 35 hours at 100° or until leathery.

REHYDRATE: Not necessary.

LEATHERS: Usually mixed with other fruit leathers for added flavor, sweetness and texture. Dry approximately 16 to 18 hours at 100°.

SPECIAL NOTES: Use in its dried form as a snack, in bakery products, in breakfast cereals or in trail mix.

DATE SUGAR

Makes: 2 cups

Date sugar is sold in health food stores as an alternative to sugar. It is substituted in recipes as a sweetener, but cannot be used as a substitute in recipes where the sugar and butter are creamed and then baked because it will not produce the proper texture.

1 lb. dried dates

Cut or chop dried dates and grind into fine pieces with a food processor, food mill or blender. Spread onto drying trays and dehydrate for several hours until dates are dry and not sticky. Grind again to a fine powder with a coffee mill.

DATE NUT BREAD

Makes: 2 loaves

This is a delicious, moist, dense bread that I like to serve with a pineapple cream cheese spread. I've used this recipe for weddings, formal parties and special teas.

2 cups boiling water
1 lb. dried dates, chopped
2 tbs. butter
2 tsp. baking soda

2 cups sugar
3½ cups flour
2 tsp. vanilla
1 cup walnuts, chopped

Preheat oven to 325°. Line bottom of 2 loaf pans with greased brown paper and grease sides of pans. Pour boiling water on chopped dates and add butter. Mix together and let cool completely. Add soda, sugar, flour, vanilla and nuts. Stir until just mixed. Pour into prepared pans and bake for 1 hour. Test by inserting a knife in center. Cool on a rack before removing from pan.

PINEAPPLE CREAM CHEESE

Makes: 2 cups

1 can (10½ oz.) crushed pineapple, drained

8 oz. cream cheese, softened
sugar to taste, optional

Simply mix pineapple and softened cream cheese together. Taste and if desired, add a small amount of sugar to sweeten. Slice bread into rectangular pieces and spread with a thick layer of pineapple cream cheese mixture.

OATMEAL DATE BARS

This great date bar is easy to make and loaded with filling.

4 cups oatmeal
4 cups flour
2 cups butter
2 cups brown sugar
2 tsp. baking soda

2 lb. dried dates, chopped
1 cup sugar
¾ cup water
¼ cup lemon juice
2 cups walnuts

Preheat oven to 350°. Grease a 9-x-13-inch pan. Using a pastry blender, mix oatmeal, flour, butter, brown sugar and soda together until crumbly. Press half crumb mixture into bottom of prepared pan. Reserve remaining crumb mixture for top layer. Place remaining ingredients in a saucepan and boil until mixture thickens. Taste and adjust filling to your personal taste. Pour mixture over pressed crumbs and top with remaining crumb mixture. Bake for 40 minutes. Let cool and then cut into squares.

STEAMED DATE PUDDING

This is my favorite holiday steamed pudding. I think it far surpasses the typical plum pudding. The cherries are a delicious surprise and go very well with an amaretto-flavored hard sauce.

1 lb. dates
1 cup boiling water
1 tsp. baking soda
½ cup butter
1 cup sugar

2 eggs
1 cup flour
1 tsp. vanilla
1 cup chopped nuts
½ large jar maraschino cherries

Chop dates and sprinkle with boiling water and baking soda. In a separate bowl, mix butter and sugar until creamed; add eggs. Add flour, soaked dates and vanilla until mixed. Stir in nuts and chopped cherries. Grease a 3-lb. coffee can and layer with waxed paper. Fill can ⅔ full with batter and cover with 2 layers of waxed paper. Set a plate in the bottom of a kettle, place can in kettle and pour boiling water ¾ way up side of can. Cover. Steam 3 hours. Let set 10 minutes before removing from tin. Serve with dollop of amaretto hard sauce.

NOTE: This dessert will freeze very well.

AMARETTO HARD SAUCE

1 cup butter
2 cups powdered sugar
1 egg yolk
4 tbs. cream
4 tbs. amaretto liqueur

Whip butter and powdered sugar together until smooth and creamy. Beat in yolk, cream and amaretto. Adjust quantity of amaretto to your personal taste.

NOTE: If you prefer a nonalcoholic sauce, consider using either almond or cherry extract instead of amaretto.

SWEET AND HOT DATE WALNUT WAFERS   Makes: 24

This is a great appetizer that you can keep in your freezer and pull out when unexpected guests arrive. Simply cut and bake and you have a sweet and spicy treat.

8 oz. grated sharp cheddar cheese
½ cup butter
1½ cups flour
¼ tsp. cayenne, or to taste
½ tsp. salt
4 tbs. white wine

6 oz. chopped dates
1 cup walnuts
1 beaten egg
ground walnuts, sesame seeds or
   Parmesan cheese for garnish

Combine cheese, butter, flour, cayenne and salt and mix with a pastry blender or food processor until mixture resembles coarse cornmeal. Add white wine. Cut in dates and walnuts and form into a log. Wrap with waxed paper or plastic wrap and chill. Cut dough into slices and brush with beaten egg. Top with either ground walnuts, sesame seeds or Parmesan cheese. Bake at 375° for approximately 10 minutes or until golden brown. Best served warm.

NOTE: This dough freezes well.

BLACK-EYED SUSANS

Makes: 3 dozen

Make these appetizers ahead of time and freeze. Whenever a drop-in guest pays a visit, pop them in the oven and wow your friends with an unusual treat.

1 cup butter
1 lb. grated sharp cheddar cheese
2 cups flour
salt to taste
cayenne to taste
1 lb. pitted dried dates
½ cup sugar (for rolling)

Cut up butter and place in a food processor. Add cheese, flour, salt and cayenne and quickly process (do not overmix). Taste and adjust to your personal taste. Roll dough into balls and press a date into center, covering it entirely with dough. Roll in sugar and place on a greased cookie sheet. Bake in a slow oven (300°) for 30 minutes.

GRAPES

PREPARATION: Use only seedless variety. Wash and remove grapes from the stem.

PRETREATMENT: Drop in boiling water for several minutes to break (or "check") the skins.

DEHYDRATE: Spread a single layer on the trays and dry approximately 80 hours at 100° or until leathery with no moisture pockets.

REHYDRATE: Not necessary, but often recipes like to plump the grapes (raisins) by soaking in hot water for about ½ hour before using.

LEATHERS: Grapes make a great fruit leather. Mix the varieties for a unique flavor. Dry approximately 16 to 18 hours at 100°.

SPECIAL NOTES: Dried grapes can be added to almost any bakery product, as well as many savory dishes. I really prefer the home-dried variety over the commercial brands. Save them for snacks and special dishes where they will be appreciated.

RAISIN COOKIES

There are a million ways to use dried grapes (raisins). This is a recipe my grandmother used to make especially for me.

2 cups dried grapes (raisins)
1 cup water
½ cup butter
½ cup margarine
2 cups sugar
3 eggs
1 cup chopped nuts

4 cups flour
1 tsp. baking powder
1 tsp. baking soda
2 tsp. salt
1½ tsp. cinnamon
½ tsp. ground dried cloves
¼ tsp. nutmeg

Preheat oven to 350°. Grease a baking sheet. In a saucepan, pour water over dried grapes (raisins) and cook on medium for 5 minutes. Cream butter, margarine and sugar together until fluffy. Add eggs and beat well. Mix in nuts. Mix flour, baking powder, baking soda, salt, cinnamon, cloves and nutmeg together, and add to creamed mixture. Mix well and drop by tablespoons onto prepared baking sheet. Bake approximately 20 minutes.

KIWI

PREPARATION: Peel the skin and slice into even ¼-inch slices.

PRETREATMENT: None necessary.

DEHYDRATE: Dry in a single layer for 48 hours at 100° or until pliable.

REHYDRATE: Pour hot water on top and soak about 20 minutes; drain. The kiwi will lose quite a bit of color.

LEATHERS: Can be used in leathers when mixed with other pureed fruits.

SPECIAL NOTES: Best when eaten in its dried state. If choosing to rehydrate, can be used in bakery products like mashed bananas.

KIWI FROZEN YOGURT

Makes: 1 quart

The kiwi in this recipe can be exchanged for other exotic dried fruits.

3/4 cup rehydrated kiwi
1 tbs. lime juice
1 tbs. dried lime peel
3/4 cup sugar
1/2 tsp. vanilla or orange extract
1 cup milk
1 cup plain yogurt
green food color, optional

Drain kiwi well before using. In a food processor or blender, puree kiwi until smooth. Add lime juice, lime peel, sugar and vanilla; mix well. Transfer ingredients to a bowl and stir in milk, yogurt and food coloring. Freeze in an ice cream maker or place mixture in a shallow dish, cover and freeze. Remove from freezer, chop up and whirl in a blender or food processor to incorporate air. Return to freezer to freeze again. If time permits, repeat this process again for a smoother frozen yogurt.

MANGO

PREPARATION: Peel, remove the seed and cut into slices.

PRETREATMENT: Not necessary.

DEHYDRATE: Lay slices in a single layer on trays and dry for approximately 20 hours at 100° or until pliable.

REHYDRATE: Soak for 1 hour in cold water.

LEATHERS: Makes excellent leather. Dry 16 to 18 hours at 100° until pliable.

SPECIAL NOTES: Mangos are best served dried. Add to granola, cereals or trail mix. If rehydrating, best used in bakery goods, cordials or chutney.

MANGO BREAD

This delicious bread was served to me with a pineapple cream cheese spread by my sister-in-law. Be creative for your next get-together and bring something surprisingly different.

2 eggs
1¼ cups sugar
¾ cup oil
2½ cups rehydrated mangos
1 tsp. lemon juice

2 cups flour
2 tsp. cinnamon
2 tsp. baking soda
½ tsp. salt
1 cup dried grapes (raisins)

Preheat oven to 350°. Line 2 loaf pans with greased brown paper and grease sides of pans. With a mixer, beat eggs; add sugar and oil and beat until smooth. Add rehydrated mangos and lemon juice and beat well. Mix flour, cinnamon, baking soda, and salt together and add to creamed mixture, beating until just mixed. Stir in dried grapes (raisins) and pour into prepared pans. Bake for 1 hour or until a knife inserted in center comes out clean.

PAPAYA

PREPARATION: Peel, slice in half, scoop out the seeds and slice into strips.

PRETREATMENT: Not necessary.

DEHYDRATE: Dry at 100° for approximately 20 hours or until pliable.

REHYDRATE: Soak in cold water for at least an hour.

LEATHERS: Good for leathers, but better when combined with other fruit purees. Dry at 100° for 16 to 18 hours.

SPECIAL NOTES: Good for snacking on when dried. Tends to be mushy when rehydrated.

MIXED FRUIT SOUP

This can be used as a starter course or a delicious dessert. You can create a totally different taste by changing the combination of dried fruits used.

2 cups water
2 slices lemon, dried or fresh
2 slices orange, dried or fresh
¼ tsp. cinnamon
pinch of cloves
2 cups chopped mixed dried fruit
1 cup water
2 cups orange juice

1 cup canned pineapple chunks,
  undrained
¼ cup honey
1 tbs. lemon juice
dash of salt
2 tbs. tapioca
whipped cream, frozen yogurt,
  flavored yogurt for garnish

Combine 2 cups water, lemon slices, orange slices, cinnamon, cloves and mixed dried fruit in a saucepan and bring to a boil. Cover, remove from heat and let steep for about 30 minutes. Mix remaining ingredients (except the garnish) together. Drain steeped fruit and remove lemon and orange slices. Add to orange juice mixture and simmer for 15 minutes. Taste and adjust seasonings to your personal taste. You may need to add more honey depending on sweetness of dried fruits used. Serve hot or chilled. Garnish with a dollop of cream or yogurt or serve over ice cream.

PEACHES

PREPARATION: Wash, scald and then dip into cold water to remove skins. Remove stone and cut into ¼-slices.

PRETREATMENT: Soak slices in ascorbic acid bath for 2 to 3 minutes.

DEHYDRATE: Lay in single slices on trays and dry at 100° for approximately 30 hours or until pliable.

REHYDRATE: Soak in cold water for 1 hour or hot water for 15 minutes and drain.

LEATHERS: Excellent for leathers. Dry at 100° for approximately 14 hours or until pliable.

SPECIAL NOTES: Good in bakery goods: pies, cobblers, chutney, cereals and trail mix.

GINGER PEACH JAM

Makes: 6 cups

If you have a large quantity of dried peaches on hand, consider turning it into a delicious jam.

3¾ cups rehydrated peaches
¼ cup lemon juice
1 to 2 oz. finely chopped candied ginger
1 pkg. powdered pectin
5 cups sugar

Chop rehydrated peaches and place in a kettle. Add lemon juice, candied ginger and pectin; stir well. Place on high heat and bring quickly to a boil, stirring constantly. Add sugar, continue stirring and heat again to a full boil. Boil hard for approximately 1 minute, stirring constantly. Remove from heat. Fill clean canning jars with jam and process in a hot water bath for 5 minutes.

PEARS

PREPARATION: Peel, core and cut into slices.

PRETREATMENT: Soak in an ascorbic acid bath for 2 to 3 minutes.

DEHYDRATE: Dry at 100° for approximately 10 hours or until leathery and pliable.

REHYDRATE: Cover with cold water for 20 minutes and drain.

LEATHERS: Puree, add 1 tsp. ascorbic acid for every 3 pears and dry at 100° for about 18 hours. Leather will have a brown color, but flavor is excellent.

SPECIAL NOTES: Dried pears are delicious and great for snacks, in bakery products, cereals, trail mix and chutneys.

MIXED FRUIT COFFEE CAKE

Servings: 12

You can add almost any combination of dried fruits to this cake batter to create a different look and flavor each time. If you use a lot of dried cherries, you might want to try using almond or cherry extracts instead of vanilla extract for a unique difference.

1½ cups mixed dried fruit
boiling water to cover
2 cups flour
2 tsp. baking powder
¼ tsp. salt
¾ cup softened butter
¾ cup sugar
1 tsp. vanilla extract (or extract of choice)

2 eggs
¾ cup milk
1 cup dark brown sugar
1 tbs. flour
1 tbs. cinnamon
½ cup chopped nuts
4 tbs. melted butter
powdered sugar for dusting top of cake

Preheat oven to 350°. Grease and flour a tube pan. Cover dried fruit of choice with boiling water and set aside for about 15 minutes. Drain well and chop fruit finely. Mix together flour, baking powder and salt and set aside.

Continued on next page

In a mixer, cream softened butter and sugar together until fluffy. Add vanilla and eggs and beat well. Add milk to creamed butter mixture alternately with flour mixture. Stir in chopped dried fruits. Combine brown sugar, flour, cinnamon and chopped nuts. Spoon ⅓ of the batter into prepared tube pan and sprinkle with half the brown sugar mixture. Drizzle 2 tbs. melted butter on top of brown sugar mixture and repeat process again. Top with remaining batter, spreading batter smoothly. Bake for about 1 hour or until a knife inserted into cake comes out clean. Cool for 15 minutes before removing from pan. Cool completely and sprinkle with powdered sugar.

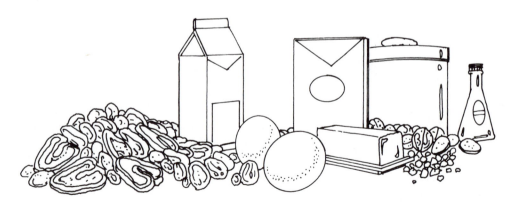

PINEAPPLE

PREPARATION: Wash, peel and remove hard core. Cut into ½-inch thick slices.

PRETREATMENT: Not necessary.

DEHYDRATE: Dry at 100° for approximately 72 hours or until leathery but not sticky. (Drying time may vary greatly depending on size of slice).

REHYDRATE: Cover with hot water and soak for about 15 minutes. Dried pineapple is most often used in its dried state.

LEATHERS: Makes an excellent leather. Dry at 100° for approximately 16 to 18 hours or until pliable but not sticky.

SPECIAL NOTES: Great in bakery goods, candies or as a snack. It is important to remember not to use fresh (noncanned) pineapple in gelatin recipes because the acid in the pineapple will prevent gelatin from setting.

PINEAPPLE NUT BREAD

Makes: 1 loaf

I think macadamia nuts and pineapple are a great combination. You can give this even a more tropical flair by adding about ½ cup dried coconut.

1½ cups sugar
½ cup butter
3 eggs
1 tsp. vanilla
½ cup pineapple juice

3 cups flour
1½ tsp. baking powder
½ tsp. salt
1 cup macadamia nuts, chopped
1 cup dried pineapple, chopped

Preheat oven to 350°. Prepare a loaf pan by lining bottom with brown paper and greasing paper and sides of pan. Cream sugar and butter together until fluffy. Add eggs, one at a time, mixing well after each. Add vanilla and pineapple juice; mix well. Mix flour, baking powder and salt together and stir into creamed mixture. Pour batter into prepared pan and bake for 1 to 1¼ hours. Test for doneness by inserting a knife in center. Remove from oven, cool for 15 minutes and remove from pan.

PLUMS

PREPARATION: Wash, halve and remove stone. Flatten by pressing together in your hands.

PRETREATMENT: Not necessary.

DEHYDRATE: Dry at 100° for approximately 72 hours or until leathery and pliable with no pockets of moisture. If you chose to cut into slices, drying time will be approximately 30 to 35 hours.

NOTE: If choosing to dry plums whole, allow about 4 times longer to dry. Be sure to check skin by dropping in boiling water for several minutes to break skins.

REHYDRATE: Either cover with cold water and soak for about 2 hours, stew in hot water or fruit juice for 10 minutes or steam about 5 minutes. Plums (or prunes) are used most often dried in recipes.

LEATHERS: Makes excellent leathers, but you may want to mix with other fruit purees because of the "laxative" effect of plums (prunes). Dry at 100° for approximately 16 to 18 hours, or until pliable but not sticky.

SPECIAL NOTES: 2½ lbs. of plums will yield about 1 lb. of dried plums (prunes). Use in both sweet and savory dishes.

WILD RICE STUFFING

This has an exotic flare with the different spicing and the addition of dried fruit. Serve with all forms of poultry and wild game dishes.

1½ cups rehydrated minced onions
¾ cup rehydrated diced celery
4 tbs. butter
12 peppercorns
6 whole cloves
1 (4-inch) cinnamon stick
2 garlic cloves
¼ tsp. ground or 6 whole pods
   cardamom

3½ cups chicken stock
1 cup wild rice
salt and pepper to taste
1 cup white rice
1 cup dried green grapes (raisins)
¼ cup diced dehydrated apricots
½ cup dehydrated plums
½ cup toasted slivered almonds

Sauté rehydrated onions and celery in butter for several minutes (until wilted). In a bouquet garni bag or cheesecloth bag, place peppercorns, cloves, cinnamon stick, garlic and cardamom. Seal bag and hit with a mallet to crush. To wilted vegetables, add chicken stock, bouquet garni bag, wild rice, salt and pepper. Cover and cook for 30 minutes. Add white rice, raisins, apricots and plums; cook an additional 15 minutes. Remove bouquet garni bag and lightly mix in toasted almonds. Taste and adjust seasonings to your personal preference.

PRUNE MAYONNAISE CAKE

Servings: 12

A very delicious moist cake. Next time, instead of prunes, use dried chopped dates with a little cinnamon for a great new taste sensation.

2 cups sifted cake flour
1 cup sugar
¼ cup cocoa powder
2 tbs. baking powder
¼ tsp. salt

1 lb. rehydrated plums (prunes)
1 cup chopped nuts
1 cup mayonnaise
1 cup cold prune water or cold water
1 tsp. vanilla extract

Preheat oven to 350°. Grease a 9-x-13-inch pan. Sift flour, sugar, cocoa, baking powder and salt together. Stir in rehydrated plums (prunes) and chopped nuts. Mix mayonnaise, leftover rehydrated plum (prune) water and mayonnaise together. Stir mayonnaise mixture into dry ingredients and blend thoroughly. Pour into prepared pan. Bake approximately 35 minutes or until cake springs back to the touch.

RHUBARB

PREPARATION: Wash, trim and slice into 1-inch pieces. Do not use the leaves as they are very poisonous.

PRETREATMENT: Not necessary. Some people like to steam rhubarb pieces for 1 to 2 minutes to guarantee tenderness.

DEHYDRATE: Dry in single layers at 100° for approximately 12 hours or until crisp.

REHYDRATE: Cover with cold water and soak for about 1 hour; drain. If using as a filling or sauce, cover with hot water and simmer until just tender.

LEATHERS: Because rhubarb is very tart, it should be mixed with other sweet fruit purees such as strawberries or apples. Dry at 100° for about 16 to 18 hours.

SPECIAL NOTES: Rhubarb has a tendency to lose color after drying but also tends to be less tart. Best used as fillings or in sauces.

RHUBARB CREAM CHEESE PIE

My sister Karen gave me this recipe. We went to a church pie social together and I liked her pie the best.

4 cups rehydrated rhubarb
3 tbs. cornstarch
1/4 tsp. salt
1 1/2 cups sugar (or more to taste)
8 oz. cream cheese

2 eggs
1/2 tsp. vanilla
1 cup sour cream
1 (9-inch) unbaked pie crust
sliced almonds for garnish

Preheat oven to 425°. In a heavy saucepan, cook rhubarb (1-inch cubes ideally), cornstarch, salt and 1 cup sugar over medium heat until mixture boils and thickens. Let mixture cool and pour into unbaked pie crust. Bake 10 minutes and remove from oven. While pie is baking, with a mixer, beat cream cheese, eggs, remaining 1/2 cup sugar and vanilla together until smooth. Pour over rhubarb mixture. Turn oven down to 350° and bake an additional 30 minutes or until set. Chill. Spread sour cream over chilled pie and garnish with sliced almonds before serving.

RHUBARB RELISH

My dear friend's mother Myrtle gave me this recipe. This sauce is great on meat dishes.

2 cups rehydrated sliced rhubarb
1 cup cider vinegar
2 cups rehydrated chopped onion
1 lb. dark brown sugar
1 tsp. celery seed
½ tsp. cinnamon
½ tsp. salt
½ tsp. pepper
1½ tsp. ground cloves

In a heavy saucepan, mix rehydrated rhubarb and vinegar together. Bring to a boil, reduce heat and simmer for about 20 minutes. Add remaining ingredients and simmer on low for 1 hour, until sauce is thick. Taste and adjust sweetness or spices to personal preference.

NECTARINES

PREPARATION: Peel, remove stone and slice.

PRETREATMENT: Dip in ascorbic acid bath for about 2 minutes and drain.

DEHYDRATE: Dry in single layers at 100° for approximately 30 hours or until leathery and pliable.

REHYDRATE: Cover with hot water, soak about 10 minutes and drain.

LEATHERS: Makes great leathers. Dry at 100° for about 18 hours or until pliable.

SPECIAL NOTES: Best eaten in its dried state. Nectarines tend to lose flavor and color with rehydrating.

NECTARINE CORDIAL

Makes: 1½ quarts

Cordials are generally served as an after-dinner drink. They make great homemade gifts.

1 lb. dried nectarines
2 cups sugar
1 cup brandy
3½ cups dry white wine

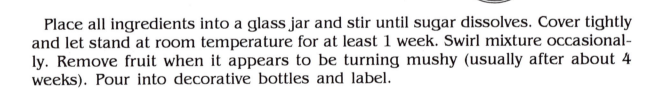

Place all ingredients into a glass jar and stir until sugar dissolves. Cover tightly and let stand at room temperature for at least 1 week. Swirl mixture occasionally. Remove fruit when it appears to be turning mushy (usually after about 4 weeks). Pour into decorative bottles and label.

STRAWBERRIES

PREPARATION: Wash, remove stems and slice into ¼-inch pieces.

PRETREATMENT: Not necessary.

DEHYDRATE: Dry in single layers at 100° for about 30 hours or until pliable and leathery.

REHYDRATE: Cover with hot water and soak for about 15 minutes. Be careful not to let soak too long or strawberries become very mushy. I prefer to add the dried fruit directly to recipes without rehydrating unless the recipe calls for mashed fruit.

LEATHERS: Strawberries make excellent leather (either by itself or mixed with other fruit purees) because of their natural sweetness and popular flavor. Dry at 100° for 16 to 18 hours.

SPECIAL NOTES: Use as a snack, in cereals like granola, and in dairy products like ice cream, milk shakes and yogurt.

STRAWBERRY BREAD

Makes: 2 loaves

A great bread for tea parties, brunches or simply as a snack. During strawberry season, I dehydrate a lot of berries and find that the rehydrated berries work best in bread or cake recipes.

3 cups flour
1 tsp. baking powder
1 tsp. salt
1 tbs. cinnamon
2 cups sugar
4 eggs
1¼ cups chopped pecans
1¼ cups melted butter
2 cups rehydrated strawberries, well drained

Mix flour, baking powder, salt, cinnamon and sugar together. Beat eggs well and add dry ingredients, pecans, butter and strawberries; mix thoroughly. Line 2 loaf pans with greased brown paper and grease sides of pans. Bake at 350° for approximately 1 hour or until a knife inserted in center comes out clean. Cool 10 minutes and turn out onto a rack. Serve with honey butter.

WATERMELON

PREPARATION: Remove rinds and seeds. Cut into ¼-inch slices.

PRETREATMENT: Not necessary.

DEHYDRATE: Dry at 100° for approximately 33 hours or until pliable.

REHYDRATE: Cover with cold water and soak about 1 hour. Tends to be mushy with rehydrating.

LEATHERS: Not recommended for leathers.

SPECIAL NOTES: Best used as a dried snack food.

FRUIT AND NUT TREATS

Makes: 2 dozen

Dried watermelon is usually eaten as is — it tastes like chewy candy. Since rehydrated watermelon loses flavor and causes a mushy texture, I prefer to use it dried in trail mixes or fruit snacks.

1½ cups mixed toasted nuts
½ cup dried watermelon
½ cup chopped dates
½ cup mixed dried grapes (raisins)
¼ cup chopped dried apples
1 tsp. lemon juice
1 to 2 tbs. dark rum
powdered sugar or shredded coconut for coating

Mix toasted nuts and chopped fruit together. Pour on lemon juice and rum (enough to make the mixture hold together). Form into small log-shaped pieces and roll in powdered sugar or coconut. Allow to air-dry for at least 24 hours.

ARTICHOKES

PREPARATION: Wash, remove leaves, discard fuzzy choke and cut heart into quarters.

PRETREATMENT: Steam for about 4 minutes.

DEHYDRATE: Dry at 100° for approximately 18 hours or until brittle.

REHYDRATE: Pour boiling water on top, add a little lemon juice to help retain the color and soak about 15 minutes; drain well.

SPECIAL NOTES: I have dried canned artichokes to take backpacking and it worked beautifully. Dried artichokes are good marinated or in appetizer dips. Keep in mind that artichokes are good for the liver, so don't neglect them in your diet.

MARINATED ARTICHOKE HEARTS

Makes: 6 cups

Most recipes call for marinated artichoke hearts. Here's a way to make your own.

2 cups dried artichoke hearts
6 cups boiling water
½ cup white wine vinegar
½ cup water
2 garlic cloves, minced
½ tsp. sugar
½ tsp. dried thyme

1 tbs. salt
1 tsp. dried basil
1 tsp. dried oregano
¼ tsp. dried red pepper flakes
½ cup olive oil
½ cup vegetable oil

Drop dried artichoke hearts into boiling water with a little lemon juice and let sit about 15 minutes (or until artichokes are tender). Drain, dry and place into small clean jars. In a saucepan, bring white wine vinegar, water, garlic, sugar and seasonings to a boil. Pour mixture over artichokes; add oils. Seal tightly and refrigerate for 1 week prior to using. This will keep, refrigerated, for 3 weeks.

NOTE: Turn jar upside down from time to time to blend the flavors.

ARTICHOKE DIP

Makes: 3½ cups

This is a quick, simple and rich recipe that people are crazy about.

15 oz. marinated artichoke hearts (see page 78)
1 cup grated Parmesan cheese
1 cup mayonnaise
½ cup diced green chiles

Drain artichokes. Mix with cheese, mayonnaise and green chiles. Pour into a small ovenproof dish and bake at 350° for 20 minutes. Serve hot with crackers.

ASPARAGUS

PREPARATION: Wash and remove tough ends.

PRETREATMENT: Steam blanch about 3 minutes.

DEHYDRATE: Dry at 100° for approximately 35 to 40 hours (depending on the size of the stalk) or until very dry and brittle.

REHYDRATE: Cover with hot water and let soak about 30 minutes. (Stems tend to remain tough.)

SPECIAL NOTES: Asparagus have a very high water content, so it requires a long drying time and needs to be very brittle to avoid molding. Best used in recipes that require mashed asparagus, or cut and mixed into a casserole dish.

PATÉ WITH ASPARAGUS

Makes: 1 loaf

Dried asparagus tends to be a little tough, so it is best used in recipes where the rehydrated asparagus is mashed or incorporated into a hot dish. This paté uses the asparagus to create an appealing color and look. Serve it with asparagus mayonnaise.

1 cup rehydrated asparagus spears
1 cup rehydrated spinach
1 lb. ground pork
1 lb. lean ground beef
1 cup fresh bread crumbs
1 tsp. dried sage

1 tsp. dried thyme
2 tsp. salt
1 tsp. pepper
1 tsp. dried rosemary
1 tbs. chopped rehydrated parsley
2 garlic cloves, minced

Preheat oven to 350°. Drain asparagus and set aside. Squeeze rehydrated spinach dry and mix with remaining ingredients. Press mixture into a loaf pan (preferably ceramic), layering rehydrated asparagus spears randomly throughout mixture. Bake for 45 minutes or until a thermometer registers 170°. Cool. Cover, place a weight on top of paté and chill overnight.

To serve: Unmold paté and place on a serving dish. Slice like a meat loaf and serve on a lettuce leaf with a dollop of asparagus mayonnaise.

ASPARAGUS MAYONNAISE

Makes: 2½ cups

Great served on patés, used in sandwiches or for dipping artichokes.

4 egg yolks
1 tbs. dry mustard
salt and pepper to taste
1 tbs. vinegar (I prefer balsamic)
1½ cups vegetable oil
½ cup rehydrated mashed asparagus

Place egg yolks, mustard, salt, pepper and vinegar in a blender or food processor and whirl to blend. With appliance running, add oil in a very thin stream until mixture thickens. Stir in asparagus. Taste and adjust seasonings.

AVOCADO

PREPARATION: Peel, remove seed and slice.

PRETREATMENT: Soak in an ascorbic acid bath for about 5 minutes; drain.

DEHYDRATE: Because of the high oil content, it takes a long time to dehydrate. Dry at 100° for approximately 60 hours or until brittle.

REHYDRATE: Pour hot water on top and let soak about 15 minutes; drain.

SPECIAL NOTES: Even with the ascorbic acid, the avocados will turn brown, but they can be used in recipes such as bakery products which call for mashed avocado.

AVOCADO BREAD

A great moist bread, this is easy to make and not affected by the color of a rehydrated avocado.

2 eggs
1 cup rehydrated avocado
1 cup buttermilk
⅔ cup oil
4 cups flour

1½ cups sugar
1 tsp. baking soda
1 tsp. baking powder
½ tsp. salt
1½ cups chopped pecans

Preheat oven to 350°. Line 2 loaf pans with greased brown paper and grease sides of pan. In a mixer or food processor, mix eggs, mashed rehydrated avocado, buttermilk and oil until well blended. Add flour, sugar, baking soda, baking powder, salt and pecans. Mix only until blended; do not overmix. Pour batter into prepared pans. Bake 1 hour or until a knife inserted in center comes out clean. Cool 10 minutes before removing from pan.

AVOCADO MAYONNAISE

Makes: 1½ cups

Can you imagine all the things you can do with an avocado mayonnaise? Serve with your favorite sandwich combinations, on patés, on salads or in appetizer dips.

¼ cup rehydrated onion
½ cup rehydrated mashed avocado
1 egg
1¼ cups vegetable oil
2 tsp. Dijon mustard
1 tsp. lemon juice
1 tsp. red wine vinegar (I prefer balsamic)
1 tsp. salt
pepper to taste
3 tbs. fresh grapefruit juice

In a food processor or blender, process onion and avocado until pureed. Add egg, 3 tbs. oil, mustard, lemon juice, vinegar, salt and pepper. Process for 15 seconds until thick. With machine running, slowly drizzle remaining oil into avocado mixture until mixture thickens. Add grapefruit juice and process to mix. Taste and adjust seasonings.

BEANS, GREEN

PREPARATION: Wash, snip off the ends and slice into segments.

PRETREATMENT: Steam blanch for about 4 minutes. Place a single layer on a tray and freeze solid (about 40 minutes) to tenderize before drying.

DEHYDRATE: Dry at 100° for approximately 30 hours or until crisp and brittle.

REHYDRATE: Soak for at least 2 hours in cold water, cover with hot water and let sit at least 1 hour, or simply add to soups and stews and let rehydrate while cooking. If adding dried vegetables to a thick stew, for example, you may need to add additional liquid.

SPECIAL NOTES: Dried green beans are best served in hot main dishes like stews, soups or casseroles.

SALAD NIÇOISE

This is a famous French salad made with a combination of green beans, tuna and potato with a delicious vinaigrette. Serve with a crusty French bread.

1 cup olive oil
2 tbs. lemon juice
4 tbs. red wine vinegar (I prefer
  balsamic)
2 tbs. Dijon mustard
2 garlic cloves, minced
1½ tsp. dried basil
1½ tsp. dried oregano
salt and pepper to taste

lettuce to line a platter
8 to 10 cooked red potatoes
½ lb. rehydrated green beans
4 to 6 sliced plum tomatoes
½ cup Greek olives
2 cans (7 oz. each) tuna
3 to 4 hard-boiled eggs
4 tbs. capers
anchovies, optional

Combine oil, lemon juice, vinegar, mustard, garlic, basil, oregano, salt and pepper together. Line a serving dish with lettuce leaves and drizzle a little vinaigrette over lettuce. Cut potatoes into slices and toss with vinaigrette. Toss vinaigrette with cooked green beans and if desired, sprinkle on a little dried tarragon for a different flavor.

Continued on next page

Arrange potatoes and green beans in concentric circles around platter. Next, working inward, circle with tomatoes, olives and sliced hard-boiled eggs. Place tuna fish, which is flaked with a fork, in center and sprinkle capers all over. If you choose to use anchovies, strategically place around the dish. Drizzle dressing over the entire salad or serve dressing alongside.

BEETS

PREPARATION: Wash and remove tops.

PRETREATMENT: If large cut in half. Steam until tender, about 20 to 30 minutes. Peel and cut into ½-inch slices.

DEHYDRATE: Dry at 100° for approximately 12 to 15 hours or until brittle.

REHYDRATE: Cover with cold water and soak for 1 hour or soak overnight in the refrigerator.

SPECIAL NOTES: Dried beets can be ground fine and used to color and flavor sauces or mix in salad dressings.

CHOCOLATE BEET CAKE

Servings: 10 to 12

The hidden ingredient in this cake is beets — they are unnoticeable in the flavor but add moisture and vitamins to this delicious cake. Just don't tell anyone they are eating beets!

3 squares unsweetened chocolate
¾ cup rehydrated beets
¼ cup beet juice (from rehydrating)
½ cup butter
2½ cup brown sugar
3 eggs
2 tsp. vanilla
½ cup buttermilk
2 cups flour
2 tsp. baking soda
½ tsp. salt

Preheat oven to 350°. Butter and flour 2 (9-inch) cake pans. Melt chocolate squares and set aside. Finely chop rehydrated beets and mix with beet juice. In a mixer, beat butter and brown sugar until creamed. Add eggs, vanilla and buttermilk and beat until mixture is well creamed. Add melted chocolate and beets and beat until well mixed. Add flour, baking soda and salt and beat well. Pour batter into prepared pans. Bake 30 minutes or until cake just barely springs back to the touch. Cool and frost.

NOTE: If batter appears somewhat thick, add a little more beet juice.

CHOCOLATE FROSTING
2 cups cream
16 oz. semisweet chocolate chips
2 tsp. vanilla

Heat cream until just boiling. Remove pan from heat and stir in chocolate chips until melted. Refrigerate mixture and stir every 10 minutes until mixture thickens like a pudding, and then stir every 5 minutes until mixture becomes thick like fudge (this will probably take 1 hour or more). At this point, frost cake and let frosting set before serving.

BEET BORSCHT

This traditional soup utilizes many rehydrated vegetables.

2 tbs. oil
2 tbs. butter
1 cup rehydrated chopped onion
1 tsp. minced garlic
3/4 lb. rehydrated shredded beets
1 cup rehydrated celery
2/3 cup chopped parsley
1 cup rehydrated grated parsnip
2 tsp. sugar
1/3 cup red wine vinegar

1 can (1 lb.) tomatoes
1 tbs. salt
3 1/2 cups diced potatoes
2 quarts beef stock or broth
1 lb. rehydrated shredded cabbage
2 cups diced cooked beef brisket
salt and pepper to taste
sour cream and chopped parsley for
   garnish

Heat oil and butter in a heavy saucepan. Add rehydrated onion and sauté about 5 minutes. Add garlic, beets, celery, parsley, parsnips, vinegar, tomatoes and salt. Cover and simmer about 30 minutes. Meanwhile, add potatoes and stock to a soup pot. Bring to a boil and simmer until potatoes are just tender. Add rehydrated cabbage, diced cooked brisket and cooked beet mixture. Bring to a boil; reduce heat and simmer about 20 minutes. Season with salt and pepper. Ladle soup into bowls and garnish with sour cream and chopped parsley.

BROCCOLI

PREPARATION: Wash and peel the tough skin from the stalk of the broccoli. Separate the florets from the stem and cut the stem on the diagonal into ½-inch slices.

PRETREATMENT: Steam blanch for about 4 minutes and drain. I've dried broccoli without pretreating and been very happy with the results.

DEHYDRATE: Dry at 100° for approximately 18 hours or until brittle.

REHYDRATE: Cover with hot water and let soak about ½ hour; drain. If planning to serve as a vegetable dish, I prefer to rehydrate with cold water, allowing a longer soaking time for a fresher-looking vegetable. Another possibility is to steam.

SPECIAL NOTES: Rehydrated broccoli is best cut up and served in a casserole dish.

CHICKEN AND BROCCOLI IN PHYLLO

Servings: 8

Don't let phyllo dough scare you. Once you get the knack of handling phyllo properly, you'll find that there are so many wonderful dishes you can create.

3 whole chicken breasts, boned
1 tbs. butter
½ rehydrated onion, chopped
1 garlic clove, minced
½ lb. rehydrated mushrooms, finely chopped
½ cup Madeira wine
salt and pepper to taste
nutmeg to taste
1 lb. rehydrated broccoli, finely chopped

2 green onions, chopped
½ cup sour cream
¼ tsp. dried thyme
¼ tsp. dried marjoram
4 egg whites
16 sheets phyllo dough
½ cup melted butter, clarified
Maderia Sauce (recipe follows)

Cut each chicken breast into 4 long strips (each portion in the phyllo will consist of 3 strips). Sauté onion and garlic in butter. Add mushrooms and sauté for several minutes. Add Madeira wine and cook until moisture evaporates. Season with salt, pepper and nutmeg and set aside. Combine broccoli with green onions, sour cream, thyme and marjoram and set aside. Beat egg whites until soft peaks form. Fold ¼ egg whites into mushrooms and the remaining egg whites into broccoli mixture.

To assemble: Use 2 sheets of phyllo per serving. Brush each piece with melted, clarified butter and stack on top of each other. Fold in half and brush again. Put 3 chicken strips across the short side of the phyllo rectangle. Top with ⅛ of each mixture. Fold sides of phyllo over filling and roll up into a neat package. Brush with butter, place on a cookie sheet and bake at 375° for 30 minutes or until browned. Top with *Madeira Sauce* and serve.

MADEIRA SAUCE
Makes: 3 cups

½ cup rehydrated chopped onion
½ cup rehydrated chopped celery
1 carrot, finely chopped
2 tbs. oil
4 tbs. butter
5 mushrooms, sliced
4 tbs. flour

1 tomato, chopped
1 tbs. tomato paste
2 cups chicken broth
½ cup Madeira
1 tbs. red currant jelly
1 bay leaf
3 peppercorns

Sauté onion, celery, and carrot in oil and butter until golden; add mushrooms and cook 4 to 5 minutes longer. Sprinkle flour over mixture and stir well. Add remaining ingredients and simmer over low heat 30 minutes. Strain and season if necessary.

ONIONS FILLED WITH BROCCOLI

Servings: 8

When I'm looking for an unusual vegetable dish, this fits the bill. It is delicious and elegant looking.

4 large yellow onions
¾ cup rehydrated broccoli, chopped
⅓ cup grated Parmesan cheese
½ cup mayonnaise
1 tsp. lemon juice
salt and pepper to taste
pimiento strip for garnish, optional

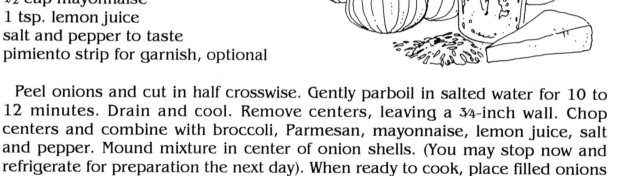

Peel onions and cut in half crosswise. Gently parboil in salted water for 10 to 12 minutes. Drain and cool. Remove centers, leaving a ¾-inch wall. Chop centers and combine with broccoli, Parmesan, mayonnaise, lemon juice, salt and pepper. Mound mixture in center of onion shells. (You may stop now and refrigerate for preparation the next day). When ready to cook, place filled onions in a shallow greased dish and bake at 375° for 20 minutes, uncovered. If desired garnish with a pimiento strip.

BRUSSELS SPROUTS

PREPARATION: Wash, remove tough outer leaves and cut in half.

PRETREATMENT: Steam blanch for about 3 minutes.

DEHYDRATE: Dry at 100° for approximately 12 to 15 hours or until brittle.

REHYDRATE: Cover with hot water and let sit about 30 minutes. You can add a little lemon juice to the water to help give it a fresher taste.

SPECIAL NOTES: Brussels sprouts seem to be either hated or loved — nothing in between. I think a cheese-flavored sauce is a nice compliment to their strong flavor.

BRUSSELS SPROUTS AND CARROTS IN MORNAY SAUCE

Servings: 8

A mornay sauce is basically a white sauce with cheese which works very well with a strong vegetable like Brussels sprouts. The carrots make a good color blend and the natural sweetness balances the slightly bitter flavor of the Brussels sprouts.

2 cups rehydrated Brussels sprouts
2 cups carrots
2 cups milk
½ onion
1 bay leaf
6 whole cloves
several blades of mace or sprinkling of nutmeg

4 tbs. butter
4 tbs. flour
salt and white pepper to taste
2 egg yolks
¼ cup cream
4 tbs. grated Parmesan cheese
4 tbs. grated Gruyère cheese

Steam Brussels sprouts and carrots until just barely tender. Rinse in cold water and set aside. Scald milk with onion piece, bay leaf, whole cloves and mace (or nutmeg). Remove from heat and let steep for a good 15 minutes. Strain out flavorings from milk and discard. Melt butter, add flour and stir for several minutes to cook flour slightly but not brown the roux. Add cooled flavored milk and stir with a whisk until thickened. Add salt and pepper to taste. Mix egg yolks and cream together. Pour a little sauce into yolk mixture and stir. Then return this mixture to remaining sauce, stirring constantly. Add ½ of the Parmesan and Gruyère cheeses to sauce and stir until cheese has melted. Place presteamed vegetables in a casserole dish and cover with cheese sauce. Sprinkle remaining cheese on top. Place under a broiler until mixture bubbles and cheese browns.

CABBAGE

PREPARATION: Wash, trim outer leaves and shred into ½-inch pieces.

PRETREATMENT: Steam-blanch for about 2 minutes.

DEHYDRATE: Dry at 100° for approximately 18 hours or until crisp.

REHYDRATE: Cover with cold water, add a little lemon juice and soak about 30 minutes.

SPECIAL NOTES: Dried cabbage is usually added to soups or stews without rehydrating.

SWEET AND SOUR CABBAGE

Servings: 6

Whole books have been written on the medicinal uses of cabbage. It's wonderful for ulcers and stomach disorders. The flavor of sweet and sour is extremely popular so that even kids enjoy this dish.

5 tbs. oil
1 lb. rehydrated sliced cabbage
1 tsp. salt
1 tbs. sugar
2 tbs. red vinegar

Heat oil in a skillet or wok. Add cabbage and stir constantly until tender-crisp. Season with salt, sugar and vinegar. Cook for about 30 seconds longer and serve immediately.

NOTE: Red vinegar can be obtained through Chinese grocers. An alternative is a good wine vinegar like balsamic to which you add some red pepper flakes or red hot sauce.

CARROTS

PREPARATION: Wash, trim tops, peel (if desired) and either cut into ¼-inch slices or shred.

PRETREATMENT: Steam blanch for about 2 minutes and drain. I have dried carrots without blanching and been very happy with the results, especially with shredded carrots.

DEHYDRATE: Dry at 100° for approximately 16 hours if using slices or 12 hours for shreds. Carrots should be brittle after drying.

REHYDRATE: Cover with cold water and let soak for about ½ hour; drain. Can be added directly to stews and soups without rehydrating.

SPECIAL NOTES: Can be made into baby food, used in bakery products or added to savory dishes like soups, casseroles and stews.

CARROT CAKE

Carrot cake is a great way to use dehydrated carrots.

3 eggs
1 cup vegetable oil
2 cups sugar
2 tsp. vanilla
2 cups flour
2 tsp. cinnamon

2 tsp. baking soda
½ tsp. salt
1½ cups rehydrated shredded carrots
1 cup crushed pineapple
1 cup coconut
1 cup walnuts

Preheat oven to 375°. Grease a 9-x-13-inch pan. With a mixer, cream eggs, oil, sugar and vanilla together. Mix flour, cinnamon, baking soda and salt together and add to egg mixture. Stir in carrots, pineapple, coconut and walnuts. Pour mixture into prepared pan. Bake for approximately 50 minutes or until a knife inserted in the center comes out clean. Cool before icing.

CREAM CHEESE ICING

3 oz. cream cheese
½ cup butter

1 box powdered sugar
1 tsp. vanilla

Cream cream cheese and butter together until smooth. Add powdered sugar and vanilla and beat until creamy. Spread on cooled cake.

CELERY

PREPARATION: Wash stalks and cut into ½-inch pieces.

PRETREATMENT: Soak celery pieces in a solution of 1 tbs. baking soda to 6 cups of cold water for 5 minutes. Then steam blanch for 2 minutes and drain. Another alternative is to simply water blanch in the soda solution for about 1 minute and drain.
NOTE: If planning to grind the celery into a powder, pretreatment is not necessary.

DEHYDRATE: Dry at 100° for approximately 18 hours or until crisp.

REHYDRATE: Cover with hot water and let soak at least an hour. Not necessary to rehydrate before using in soups or stews.

SPECIAL NOTES: Dried celery is best used in soups and stews.
- To make celery flakes - chop the dried pieces in a blender.
- To make celery salt - mix equal parts of salt and finely ground dried celery together.

VEGETABLE SOUP

Endless combinations of vegetables can be used for this versatile soup. Be inventive with the seasoning and you'll never tire of this recipe.

2 cups boiling water
2 cups mixed dried vegetables
½ cup dried onion
½ cup dried celery
3 cups broth
16 oz. crushed canned tomatoes
¾ cup barley, wheat berries or pasta
  of choice

salt and pepper to taste
1 garlic clove, minced
½ tsp. dried basil
½ tsp. dried thyme
1 tbs. dried parsley
3 to 4 tbs. butter

Pour boiling water over 2 cups of dried vegetables and set aside for at least 30 minutes. Pour boiling water over onion and celery (if dried) to rehydrate and set aside. Heat broth and tomatoes together and add barley (or starch of your choice). Add seasonings and boil for 30 minutes. Melt butter in a skillet and sauté rehydrated onion and celery until wilted. Add to cooked mixture. Add rehydrated mixed vegetables and cook for about 20 minutes. Taste and adjust seasonings to your personal preference.

STUFFED PRAWNS

A fantastic appetizer or main course for an elegant party. Rehydrated onion and celery are great in all kinds of stuffings.

16 large prawns
1/4 lb. additional prawns
1 cup rehydrated mushrooms
2/3 cup rehydrated onions
2/3 cup rehydrated celery
2 tbs. butter

1/2 tsp. minced garlic
salt and pepper to taste
3/4 cup fresh bread crumbs
1/4 cup finely chopped parsley
1 egg, lightly beaten
3 tbs. melted butter

Peel and devein 16 prawns. Chop remaining 1/4 lb. prawns and set aside. Finely chop rehydrated mushrooms, onions and celery. Heat 2 tbs. butter in a saucepan, add chopped onions, celery and garlic; cook until wilted. Add mushrooms and cook for 3 minutes. Add salt and pepper to taste. Remove mixture from heat and add chopped prawns, about 3/4 of the bread crumbs, parsley and egg. Stir to blend and season to taste. Butterfly whole prawns by splitting down the back, almost, but not all the way, through. Open them up split side down on a buttered baking dish. Spoon equal portions of stuffing on top of each prawn. Sprinkle dish with remaining bread crumbs and drizzle with 3 tbs.

melted butter. Place baking dish on lower rack of a 350° oven cook for 2 to 3 minutes until juices are heated through (this will cook the bottom side of the prawns). Then place the dish under the broiler, about 5 inches from the element. Cook for approximately 5 minutes, or until prawns are nicely browned. Do not overcook.

WILD RICE PILAF

This is a favorite pilaf recipe for special occasions. For a more exotic flare, add a few raisins.

1½ cups wild rice
1½ cups white rice
6½ cups chicken stock or water
1 lb. bacon
1½ cups rehydrated chopped onions

2 cups rehydrated chopped celery
½ cup loosely-packed chopped parsley
¾ cups toasted pine nuts
salt and pepper to taste

Cook rices separately, each in 3¼ cups chicken stock or water. Chop bacon into small pieces and fry until crisp. Remove bacon from pan and drain off most fat. Reserve a little to fry onions and celery until tender. Add parsley, cooked rices and pine nuts. Season to taste with salt and pepper. Serve immediately.

NOTE: If you are making this ahead of time, add pine nuts just before serving.

CORN

PREPARATION: Husk ears and remove silk.

PRETREATMENT: Steam blanch the corn on the cob for about 4 minutes. Use a sharp knife and cut the kernels off the cob.

DEHYDRATE: Dry at 100° for approximately 18 hours or until crisp.

REHYDRATE: Cover with hot water, let soak about 30 minutes and drain.

SPECIAL NOTES: Use dried corn in soups, chowder, creamed corn, stews or casseroles.

- To make cornmeal - simply grind dried corn kernels in a grinder or food mill.

CORN STUFFED SQUASH

Servings: 4 to 6

This is a delicious Mexican vegetable dish that is easy to make and very colorful.

1½ lbs. whole zucchini
2 cups rehydrated corn
2 eggs
2 tbs. cream
1 garlic clove
4 chopped green onions
½ tsp. dried oregano

½ tsp. cumin
salt to taste
6 oz. grated Muenster or mild
  cheddar cheese
3 tbs. softened butter
salsa sauce for garnish

Preheat oven to 350°. Butter a shallow ovenproof dish just large enough to fit the zucchini in a single layer. Clean and trim zucchini. Cut in half lengthwise and scoop out inner flesh, leaving a shell about ½-inch thick. Place zucchini in prepared baking dish. In a food processor or blender, blend corn, egg, cream, garlic, green onions, oregano, cumin and salt to a coarse puree. Mix about ¾ of the cheese into puree (save remaining cheese for topping). Fill zucchini shells with corn puree (mixture will be quite runny). Dot with butter and sprinkle remaining cheese on top. Cover dish with foil and bake until zucchini is tender, about 50 minutes. Serve covered with salsa sauce.

NOTE: Adding fresh chopped cilantro to bottled salsa improves the flavor.

EGGPLANT

PREPARATION: Simply wash and cut into ½-inch pieces.

PRETREATMENT: Not necessary. (It actually turns darker when dipped in an ascorbic acid).

DEHYDRATE: Dry at 100° for approximately 20 hours or until leathery.

REHYDRATE: Cover with hot water, soak about ½ hour and drain.

SPECIAL NOTES: Great to use in casseroles.

MOUSSAKA

Moussaka is one of my favorite lamb dishes. Eggplant is not always a popular vegetable but this dish will change even your kids' minds!

2 lb. ground lamb
3 small onions, minced
½ cup flour
½ cup lamb fat or butter
2 cup chicken stock
dash of Worcestershire sauce
¼ cup tomato paste

salt and pepper to taste
4 cups *Bechamel Sauce* (recipe follows)
2 cups grated cheese (Jack or Swiss)
4 egg yolks, beaten
4 to 6 potatoes
2 eggplants (rehydrated)

Fry lamb, saving ½ cup of fat, and brown minced onions. Heat reserved lamb fat and add flour, making a roux. Add chicken stock and stir with a whisk until smooth. Add Worcestershire sauce, tomato paste, salt and pepper. Taste and adjust seasoning to personal preference. Make *Bechamel Sauce*. Add egg yolks and grated cheese, reserving ½ cup cheese for top,) to *Bechamel Sauce* and stir until cheese is melted. Stir sauce into browned lamb mixture. Peel potatoes, slice thin and fry in a little oil or butter until colored. Rehydrate dried eggplants and brush with oil. Place under a broiler and brown. Butter a deep casserole dish and layer eggplant, meat sauce and potatoes in that order. Repeat one more set of layers, sprinkle top with reserved ½ cup cheese and bake at 350° for 30 to 40 minutes.

NOTE: Depending on your personal preference, you may want to reduce sauce slightly.

BECHAMEL SAUCE

Makes: 4 cups

4 cups milk
½ small onion, cut into large chunks
few blades of mace
2 slices of carrot
1 bay leaf

1 sprig thyme
few parsley stalks
4 tbs. butter
6 tbs. flour
salt and white pepper to taste

Put milk, onion, mace, carrot, bay leaf, thyme and parsley stalks into a saucepan and bring almost to a boil. Cover and remove from heat to allow flavorings to infuse. Set aside for at least 15 minutes. In a heavy saucepan, melt butter over medium heat, add flour and cook for 2 to 3 minutes, allowing roux to bubble. Strain milk and add to roux, stirring constantly. Allow mixture to boil for 2 to 3 minutes to thicken and make certain it doesn't have a floury taste. Taste and season with salt and white pepper to your personal preference.

EGGPLANT CAVIAR

Makes: 4 cups

Eggplant caviar was the "in" food a few years back. I would like to reinstall its popularity because it is a great all-vegetable dip for this new age of health.

equivalent of 1 eggplant (rehydrated)
⅓ cup olive oil
¾ cup rehydrated chopped onion
2 garlic cloves, minced
1 green pepper, finely chopped
2 large tomatoes

2 tbs. balsamic vinegar
1 tsp. salt
½ tsp. pepper
½ to 1 tsp. sugar
sliced olives, capers, chopped green
    olives, optional

Chop eggplant finely. Heat olive oil in a heavy skillet. Add chopped eggplant, onions, garlic and green pepper. Cover and simmer for about 10 minutes. Add remaining ingredients and simmer, covered, for 10 minutes. At this point, taste, adjust seasonings and add optional ingredients to your personal taste. Remove from heat and chill for several hours before serving. Serve with crackers, French bread or thin small bread rounds.

GINGER ROOT

PREPARATION: Peel the ginger root and slice into uniform pieces.

PRETREATMENT: Not necessary.

DEHYDRATE: Dry in single layers for approximately 18 hours at 100° or until brittle.

REHYDRATE: Pour boiling water over and let soak for 1 to 2 hours.

SPECIAL NOTES: How often have you used ginger root in recipes and wondered what to do with the remaining part? I like to keep dehydrated ginger root on hand to avoid waste.
- 1 tsp. rehydrated minced ginger root equals ½ tsp. ground ginger powder

TIP: If you don't like to cook fish because it makes the house smell, try putting a few pieces of rehydrated ginger root around the edges of the baking dish and the room will smell of ginger instead.

CANDIED GINGER

Makes: 1½ cups

Candied ginger is great mixed with cream cheese for an appetizer or simply cut up and sprinkled on ice cream.

1 cup rehydrated sliced ginger root
1 cup water
½ cup maple syrup

In a saucepan, simmer rehydrated ginger, water and syrup together until liquid completely evaporates, approximately 20 minutes. Watch mixture carefully so it won't scorch. Remove from heat and spread on a greased drying tray, separating pieces. Dry at 100° for approximately 6 to 10 hours or until pieces become brittle.

LEEKS

PREPARATION: Cut off tough top part of leek. Then cut stalk in half and wash under running cold water to remove all dirt between layers. Cut into ¼-inch slices and separate.

PRETREATMENT: Not necessary.

DEHYDRATE: Dry at 100° for approximately 18 hours or until crisp.

REHYDRATE: Cover with hot water, soak at least 30 minutes and drain. Does not need to be rehydrated before adding to soups or stews.

SPECIAL NOTES: Dried leeks work well in cooked savory dishes like casseroles, soups and stews.

CREAM OF LEEK WITH BRIE SOUP

Servings: 8

This is a delicious smooth soup that has the unusual ingredient Brie added for a rich creaminess.

½ cup butter
3 cups rehydrated chopped leeks
2 garlic cloves, minced
½ lb. sliced mushrooms
⅓ cup flour
1 quart chicken broth
2 cups half and half
2 tsp. dried tarragon
salt and pepper to taste
8 oz. Brie cheese

In a large soup kettle, melt butter and sauté rehydrated leeks and garlic until soft. Add mushrooms and cook until limp. Sprinkle flour over cooked vegetables and stir to mix. Add chicken broth and stir until thickened. Add half and half and season to taste with tarragon, salt and pepper. Bring soup to a gentle boil and stir in cheese until melted. Serve hot.

MUSHROOMS

PREPARATION: Wash quickly and slice. (Mushrooms absorb water like a sponge, so don't leave them in soaking in water).

PRETREATMENT: Not necessary.

DEHYDRATE: Dry at 100° for approximately 18 hours or until crisp.

REHYDRATE: Cover with cold water, soak about ½ hour and drain. Not necessary to rehydrate before adding to soups or stews.

SPECIAL NOTES: Excellent in spaghetti sauce, creamed dishes, all types of savory casseroles or stuffing recipes.

INDIAN CHICKEN TRIANGLES

Makes: 4 dozen

This delicious appetizer has an East Indian flare. Use this technique with the phyllo dough and vary the filling by experimenting with different spices to create endless varieties.

2 tbs. butter
½ cup rehydrated chopped onions
¾ cup rehydrated chopped mushrooms
1 lb. poached chicken
1 tsp. cumin
salt and pepper to taste
2 tbs. rehydrated parsley
1 pkg. phyllo dough
1 lb. melted butter

Melt 2 tbs. butter in a skillet. Sauté onions and mushrooms until limp. Finely dice poached chicken. Add cumin, salt, pepper and parsley. Season to taste. Clarify butter by allowing melted butter to stand so that it separates. Skim off top layer, pour off center layer and discard bottom layer. The center layer is the true clarified butter which is best to use with phyllo dough so that dough does not brown too quickly. Unwrap phyllo dough and unroll. Cover with a slightly damp towel while working with each individual piece. (This will prevent the dough from drying out.)

Lightly butter 1 piece of dough and cut into approximately 4-inch strips. Fold strip in half lengthwise and butter it. Place a rounded teaspoon of filling in one corner of strip and fold corner-to-corner (like folding a flag), folding open edges so filling is well sealed. Fold in this manner until the last triangle fold can be made. Cut off any excess dough. Brush with butter and place on a jelly roll pan. (It is important to place pastry on a sided pan so butter that will ooze out during the baking process won't drip out into the oven.) Bake in a 350° oven for 20 minutes or until brown. Serve warm.

MUSHROOM BISQUE

My sister-in-law introduced me to this soup and I think it's marvelous.

1/4 lb. fresh mushrooms
1 tbs. butter
1 tsp. lemon juice
1/2 cup rehydrated chopped onions
1 1/2 lb. rehydrated mushrooms slices
1/2 cup butter
1 quart chicken stock

6 tbs. flour
3 cups milk
1 cup cream
1 tsp. salt
dash of Tabasco
freshly ground pepper to taste
sherry, optional

Slice fresh mushrooms and sauté in 1 tbs. butter and lemon juice until limp. Save for garnish. Finely chop onions and rehydrated mushrooms. In a large soup kettle, melt 2 tbs. butter and sauté onion until soft. Add mushrooms and stir well. Add chicken stock and cover. Simmer for 20 minutes. In a large pan, heat remaining 6 tbs. butter and add flour, stirring to form a roux. Heat milk and add to roux; stir until thickened. Add mushrooms and chicken stock mixture and stir until smooth. Add cream, salt, Tabasco and pepper. Taste and adjust seasoning to your personal preference. Just before serving, swirl a small amount of sherry in each soup bowl and garnish with sautéed mushroom slices.

ONIONS

PREPARATION: Remove paper shell and either slice or dice.

PRETREATMENT: Not necessary.

DEHYDRATE: Dry at 100° for approximately 20 hours or until brittle.

REHYDRATE: Cover with hot water, soak for about 15 minutes, and drain. Not necessary to rehydrate before adding to soups or stews.

SPECIAL NOTES: Add dried onions to hot savory dishes or rehydrate ahead of time. Be aware that dehydrating onions will make the house smell strongly.
- To make onion flakes or powder - simply place the dried onion in a blender, grinder or food mill and process until ground to desired size.
- To make onion salt - mix equal parts of salt and finely ground onion powder together.

HONEY LAMB PUFFS

Makes: 32 puffs

Here's a winning new appetizer idea. Puff pastry can now be purchased in sheets in the frozen food section of the grocery store. Use this technique with the dough and vary the fillings. Ground lamb gives this a unique flavor with a Mid-Eastern flare.

⅓ cup dried grapes (raisins)
¼ cup olive oil
1½ cups rehydrated chopped onion
1 tbs. minced garlic
1 lb. ground lamb
2 tsp. salt
1½ tsp. pepper
1 tsp. cinnamon
⅛ tsp. cayenne pepper
¼ cup tomato paste
1 cup chopped tomato
⅓ cup honey
1 pkg. frozen puff pastry (2 sheets)

Cover dried grapes (raisins) with hot water to plump. Heat olive oil and sauté onions and garlic. Add lamb, salt, pepper, cinnamon, cayenne and pepper. Cook until lamb is no longer pink. Drain off excess fat. Add tomato, drained grapes and honey. Simmer to combine flavors. Taste to correct seasoning balance. Cool. Defrost frozen puff pastry until just pliable to the touch. (Try to work quickly so that dough doesn't get too hot from your hands.) Cut each pastry sheet into 16 squares. Line miniature muffin tins with puff pastry squares by simply pushing squares in cups. The four corners should stick up. Place 2 tsp. of cooled filling in each tin. Bake at 375° for approximately 20 minutes or until pastry is golden brown. Serve warm or cool.

NOTE: These can make ahead and frozen unbaked.

RED ONION FOCCACIA

Foccacia is a delicious flavored bread that can be served as an appetizer or with a meal. It fills the house with a marvelous aroma.

2 tsp. yeast
1 cup warm water
1 tsp. sugar
2½ cups flour
½ tsp. salt
1 tbs. olive oil
1¾ lb. rehydrated sliced red onions
⅓ cup olive oil
1 tsp. anchovy paste
1 tbs. white vinegar
olive oil for brushing
salt and pepper to taste

In a nonmetal bowl, dissolve yeast in warm water. Add sugar and approximately 1 cup flour to dissolved yeast and beat vigorously for 1 minute. This mixture should be the consistency of cake batter. Cover bowl with plastic wrap and let mixture become sponge in a warm place for approximately 30 minutes. Beat mixture down and add salt, 1 tbs. olive oil and remaining flour. Knead dough for about 10 minutes. Let dough rest for 15 minutes.

Add rehydrated onion slices and ⅓ cup olive oil to a fry pan and cook over medium heat until softened. Dissolve anchovy paste in vinegar and add to onions. Cook over medium heat until onions are soft and liquid has evaporated; cool.

Punch down dough and spread on a greased 12-inch pizza pan. Let rise 30 minutes in a warm place. Brush dough lightly with olive oil and sprinkle with salt and pepper. Taste onions; add salt and pepper to taste. Spread onion mixture on dough within ½-inch of edge. Bake in a 400° oven for approximately 30 minutes or until lightly browned. Cut into wedges and serve while warm.

PARSNIPS

PREPARATION: Wash, peel and cut into ¼-inch slices.

PRETREATMENT: Steam blanch for about 4 minutes and drain.

DEHYDRATE: Dry at 100° for approximately 16 to 18 hours or until tough and brittle.

REHYDRATE: Cover with hot water, soak at least 1 hour and drain.

SPECIAL NOTES: Parsnips are wonderful mashed, in cream sauces, stews and casseroles.

PUREED PARSNIPS

Parsnips as a general rule are overlooked vegetables, but they have a wonderful, natural sweet flavor. I like to serve these as an alternative to mashed potatoes or stuffed in a steamed vegetable like zucchini.

2 lbs. dried parsnips
boiling water
6 to 8 tbs. cream
2 tbs. butter
salt and pepper to taste
nutmeg to taste

Pour boiling water over dried parsnips to cover, and cook until parsnips are very tender. Then using a vegetable mill or food processor, puree until smooth. Beat in cream, butter and seasonings to taste. Return mixture to a double boiler and continue to simmer, covered, for about 25 minutes. The texture and flavor changes considerably with additional cooking. Correct seasonings before serving.

PEAS

PREPARATION: Shell.

PRETREATMENT: Steam blanch for 3 minutes.

DEHYDRATE: Dry at 100° for approximately 12 hours or until brittle and shriveled.

REHYDRATE: Cover with hot water and soak about 30 minutes.

SPECIAL NOTES: Good mixed in hot savory dishes like stews, soups and casseroles.

PEAS AND RICE WITH SHRIMP

Servings: 6

This was served to me by a wonderful Italian cook — this dish is a nice alternative to potatoes.

4 tbs. oil
4 tbs. butter
½ cup rehydrated minced onion
1½ cups pearl rice
3 tbs. white wine
3 cups chicken broth

1 tsp. salt
1½ cups rehydrated peas
¾ lb. shrimp
1 garlic clove
2 tbs. butter
¼ cup Parmesan cheese

Heat oil and butter in a saucepan and sauté rehydrated onions for about 5 minutes. Mix in rice and cook until rice appears translucent. Add wine and cook 1 minute. Add 1½ cups broth and cook until broth is absorbed. Add peas and 1 cup broth, cooking until absorbed. Add remaining broth if needed. Meanwhile, sauté shrimp and garlic in 2 tbs. butter only until warmed. Save some for top and add remaining to rice mixture. Lastly add Parmesan by mixing gently (if rice is too dry add more broth). Sprinkle top with remaining shrimp and serve.

SPAGHETTI CARBONARA

Servings: 6 to 8

Pasta is a great way to get children to eat vegetables. This makes a side dish that is appreciated by all.

2 lb. diced bacon
1½ lb. pasta
4 tbs. butter
3 garlic cloves, minced
4 eggs
½ tsp. red pepper flakes
⅓ cup grated Romano cheese
¾ cup grated Parmesan cheese
1 cup rehydrated peas

Fry bacon until crisp, drain on paper towels and discard fat. Cook pasta, rinse in cold water and drain. Heat butter in a large skillet, add garlic and cook slightly (do not brown). Add cooked pasta. Beat eggs in a separate bowl, add pepper flakes, 2 tbs. Romano cheese and 2 tbs. Parmesan cheese. Pour this mixture over pasta and toss to mix. Cook for several minutes. Just before serving, add peas and fried bacon. Sprinkle on remaining cheese and serve immediately.

PEPPERS (GREEN OR RED)

PREPARATION: Wash, remove seeds, and either slice or dice.

PRETREATMENT: Not necessary.

DEHYDRATE: Dry at 100° for approximately 24 hours or until brittle.

REHYDRATE: Cover with hot water, soak at least 20 minutes and drain.

SPECIAL NOTES: Best in cooked savory dishes such as soups, stews or casseroles.

ROASTED RED PEPPER DIP

Makes: 2½ cups

This is a simple dip that can be ideal for the holidays. Serve this red dip with a plate of red, white and green vegetables and wow your guests. Garnish with herbs and vegetables for great eye appeal.

¾ cup rehydrated red peppers
2 chopped green onions
1 to 2 tbs. lemon juice
1 cup whipped cream cheese

Drain red peppers and place under a broiler for a few minutes until peppers are slightly browned. Using the steel blade of a food processor, finely mince green onions. Add remaining ingredients and process to make a coarse puree. Chill. Prepare a selection of beautiful fresh vegetables to serve with this dip.

STUFFED BRIE

This is a delicious and colorful appetizer that can be served year-round, but is ideal for Christmas if you use red and green dried bell peppers. Serve with a crusty French bread.

½ cup rehydrated chopped onions
1 tbs. butter
2 garlic cloves, minced
8 large mushrooms, finely chopped
½ cup rehydrated bell peppers (red and green)

4 oz. sliced black olives
1 tbs. dry sherry or white wine
dash salt and pepper
1 large Brie wheel, sliced in half horizontally

In a small skillet, sauté garlic and rehydrated onions in butter until tender. Add mushrooms, rehydrated peppers and olives; cook 3 minutes longer. Add sherry or wine and season to taste. Cool. One hour before serving, spread filling in center of Brie, reserving ½ cup of filling to garnish top. Sprinkle remaining ½ cup of filling in a circle near outer edge of Brie wheel. Serve with French bread.

SEAFOOD AND RED PEPPER MOUSSE

Servings: 10

This wonderful, rich mousse appetizer can be very elegant depending on the type of seafood you choose. Garnish the top of the mousse with a bit of the seafood and parsley.

2 tbs. unflavored gelatin
3/4 cup cold water
1 cup boiling water
3/4 cup rehydrated red pepper
1 chopped small red onion
1 cup mayonnaise

1/4 tsp. cayenne
1 tbs. lemon juice
1 cup heavy cream
2 cups mixed seafood (crabmeat, lobster, shrimp or white fish)

Dissolve gelatin in cold water, add boiling water and chill until syrupy. Broil rehydrated red peppers until slightly brown. Chop red peppers and onions in a processor or blender until pureed. Add mayonnaise and chilled gelatin. Fold in cayenne and lemon juice. Whip cream and fold into mixture. Add seafood and fold into mixture. Taste and adjust seasoning to your personal preference. Pour mixture into an oiled 6-cup mold and chill at least 4 hours or overnight. Serve with an assortment of crackers.

POTATOES

PREPARATION: Peel, wash and cut into ¼-inch slices, dice or grate.

PRETREATMENT: Soak in ascorbic acid bath or lemon juice for several minutes; drain.

DEHYDRATE: Dry at 100° for approximately 8 hours or until crisp.

REHYDRATE: Cover with cold water and let soak about 30 minutes, drain and dry before using in casseroles.

SPECIAL NOTES: Without pretreatment, potatoes will turn very black. Great for layered potato dishes like scalloped potatoes or added to casserole dishes. Grated potatoes can be used for hash browns.

LOXSLODA

Next time you are asked to bring a potato dish, consider this recipe — the loxs make it extra special.

4 cups rehydrated sliced potatoes
salt and pepper to taste
¼ cup minced onions
¼ to ½ lb. loxs
2 cups heavy cream

Butter a low, flat casserole dish. Place ⅓ of the rehydrated potatoes in casserole dish, sprinkle with salt and pepper, top with ½ of the onions and then ½ of the loxs. Repeat layers again and top with remaining potatoes. Pour on cream and cover with foil. Bake at 350° for 1 hour.

NOTE: Avoid using too much onion because it will curdle the cream.

CLAM CHOWDER

Makes: 3 quarts

This is a simple, easy chowder and a great way to use dehydrated potatoes. Serve it with crusty French bread and a tossed salad.

3 cans (10½ oz. each) minced clams
½ lb. lean salt pork, diced
1 cup rehydrated chopped onions
3 cups diced rehydrated potatoes
1 tsp. salt
¼ tsp. white pepper

2 cups half and half
2 cups milk
2 tbs. butter
½ tsp. thyme, optional
paprika for garnish

Strain clams and reserve liquid. Measure clam liquid and add water to make 4 cups of liquid. Fry salt pork in a large kettle until golden. Remove pork and reserve. Drain off all but ¼ of the fat. Add onions and sauté for 5 minutes. Add rehydrated potato, salt, pepper and reserved clam liquid with water. Simmer until potatoes are tender. Add clams, cream, milk, butter and thyme if desired. Reheat, but do not boil. Sprinkle with paprika and serve.

POTATO CHEESE BAKE

Servings: 6 to 8

I'm always looking for new ways to do potatoes. These are simple and good.

1½ lbs. rehydrated sliced potatoes
3 garlic cloves, minced
4 oz. shredded Gruyère or Swiss cheese
salt and white pepper to taste
nutmeg to taste
2 cups chicken stock

Layer potatoes with garlic, cheese and seasonings in a well-buttered casserole dish. Pour chicken stock over potatoes and bake at 400° for 45 minutes or until potatoes are fork-tender.

RADISHES

PREPARATION: Wash, trim and slice.

PRETREATMENT: Not necessary.

DEHYDRATE: Dry at 100° for approximately 15 hours or until crisp.

REHYDRATE: Cover with cold water for about ½ hour; drain.

SPECIAL NOTES: There are not many uses for dried radish other than to add spiciness to cooked dishes.

SWEET AND SOUR RADISH SALAD

Makes: 1½ cups

Rehydrated radishes lose a little color and texture when rehydrated. Mixing them with a marinade, salad dressing or light sauce helps to disguise them.

1½ cups rehydrated radishes
salt to taste
3 tbs. sugar
3 tbs. vinegar (I prefer balsamic)
1 tbs. light soy sauce
2 tbs. sesame oil

Drain radishes and sprinkle with salt. Let set for about 20 minutes. Mix sugar, vinegar, soy and sesame oil together and pour over salted radishes. Toss. Taste and adjust seasonings. Chill before serving.

SPINACH

PREPARATION: Wash well and remove stems.

PRETREATMENT: Not necessary. I have found that the spinach is far better if it is not steamed ahead of time.

DEHYDRATE: Dry at 100° for approximately 10 to 12 hours or until crisp and crumbly.

REHYDRATE: Cover with hot water, soak about 15 minutes and drain. Sometimes adding a little lemon juice to the water will freshen the flavor.

SPECIAL NOTES: There are endless savory recipes which use spinach. Always squeeze the spinach dry before using in recipes.

SPINACH STUFFED MUSHROOMS

Servings: 8 to 12

Stuffed mushrooms are great healthy appetizers to serve. Be sure to squeeze the spinach very dry after rehydrating so that the filling does not leach too much liquid while baking.

2 tbs. butter
3 tbs. minced onion
1 cup rehydrated spinach
½ cup ricotta cheese

¼ cup grated Parmesan cheese
salt and pepper to taste
grated nutmeg to taste
large mushrooms

Heat butter in a skillet. Add minced onions and sauté until onion becomes limp. Add well-squeezed rehydrated spinach, ricotta cheese, Parmesan cheese, and season to taste with salt, pepper and nutmeg. Cut stems off mushrooms just at the rim instead of just breaking the whole stem off (this helps the mushroom keep its shape). Mound the filling in the center of each and bake at 350° for approximately 20 minutes.

STUFFED CHICKEN BREASTS

Makes: 8

Stuffing is a great way to use dehydrated vegetables. Instead of just plain fried chicken, consider stuffing the breast with a wonderful spinach, bacon and onion mixture.

8 half chicken breasts
½ lb. bacon
1 cup rehydrated chopped onion
1 cup rehydrated spinach
1 egg

½ cup fresh bread crumbs
¼ cup grated Parmesan cheese
1 tbs. chopped pimientos
salt and pepper to taste
2 to 3 tbs. melted butter

Leave skin on chicken breast, but remove bone. Cut bacon into small pieces, fry until brown and drain on paper towels. Remove all but 2 tablespoons of bacon fat from the pan and sauté rehydrated chopped onion until tender. Squeeze spinach until dry and chop finely. Combine spinach, onion, bacon, egg, bread crumbs, Parmesan cheese and pimientos together. Taste; add salt and pepper to your personal preference. Lift skin from each breast half and fill with ⅛ of the stuffing mixture. Fold edges under to make a compact bundle. Brush with melted butter and place in a greased baking dish. Bake at 350° for approximately 25 minutes, or until done. Serve warm or at room temperature.

TOMATOES

PREPARATION: Wash, remove stem and slice.
- For beefsteak tomatoes - cut into ½-inch slices.
- For plum tomatoes - slice in half lengthwise and place cut side down on the tray.

PRETREATMENT: Not necessary.

DEHYDRATE: Dry at 100° for approximately 24 hours or until crisp for beefsteak tomatoes and 72 hours for plum tomato halves.

REHYDRATE: Cover beefsteak slices with cold water for about 15 minutes; drain. Cover plum tomato halves with cold water and let sit at least 30 minutes.

SPECIAL NOTES: Dried beefsteak tomatoes are not terribly appetizing when rehydrated, so I prefer to use them in sauces, stews and casseroles. Plum tomatoes are great for marinating and using in pasta dishes, salads or casseroles.

MOCK SUN-DRIED TOMATOES

Sun-dried tomatoes are extremely popular. Dried plum tomatoes are the next best things to sun-dried and make great marinated tomatoes which can be used in pasta dishes, salads, omelets or savory hot dishes.

1 lb. dried plum tomato halves
1 tsp. dried basil
1 tsp. minced garlic
pepper to taste
6 juniper berries or sprig of rosemary, optional
olive oil to cover

Pack dried tomatoes, basil, garlic, pepper and (if desired) juniper berries or rosemary in a large glass sealable jar. Cover with olive oil, seal and place in a dark cool place for ideally 1 month. When ready to use, drain off excess olive oil and cut tomatoes into strips.

LAMB STEW

This particular stew has a Mid-Eastern flare and following tradition, I like to serve this over steamed couscous. You may prefer rice.

1½ lb. stewing lamb
2 tbs. oil
1 medium onion, chopped
2 cups rehydrated tomato
2 cloves garlic, minced
1 tsp. ground dried ginger
1 tsp. fennel seed, optional
1 tsp. red pepper sauce, or to taste

1 tsp. turmeric
2 tbs. garbanzo beans
1½ cups water
2 carrots
1 zucchini
6 to 8 small new potatoes
salt and pepper to taste

Cut stewing lamb into cubes. Heat oil in a heavy, large pan and add lamb and onions. Cook on medium for about 15 minutes. Dice tomatoes and add to meat mixture along with garlic, ginger, fennel, red pepper sauce, turmeric, garbanzo beans and water. Bring to a boil, reduce heat and simmer for 1 hour. Cut carrots and zucchini into large chunks. Depending on size of potatoes, either leave whole or cut into smaller pieces. Add to stew and continue simmering for 20 minutes. Add salt and pepper to taste. Serve over steamed couscous or rice.

ZUCCHINI

PREPARATION: Wash and cut into ¼-inch slices or grate.

PRETREATMENT: Not necessary.

DEHYDRATE: Dry at 100° for approximately 12 hours or until tough and brittle.

REHYDRATE: Cover with hot water and let soak about ½ hour; drain.

SPECIAL NOTES: Grated zucchini is great in bakery products like zucchini bread or cake. The slices work well in casserole dishes. Slices can be seasoned before drying and used as a chip for snacking.

WHOLE WHEAT VEGETARIAN PIZZA

Makes: 1 pizza

Here is a healthy alternative to a favorite food that is really appreciated by kids.

CRUST

1 pkg. yeast
1 tsp. sugar
1 cup warm water
1½ cups white flour

1 cup whole wheat flour
1 tsp. salt
1 tbs. olive oil

Dissolve yeast in warm water. Add sugar and enough white flour to make a sponge (should be the consistency of pancake batter). Let rise for 30 minutes in a warm place. Beat risen sponge down with a spoon and add remaining flour and salt. If using a food processor, process until a ball of dough forms, add oil and process for an additional 40 seconds. Otherwise use either a mixer with a dough attachment or knead by hand until smooth. Let dough rest for about 10 minutes. Spread dough on a pizza pan.

TOPPING

1 cup rehydrated sliced zucchini
1 cup rehydrated sliced mushrooms
½ cup rehydrated sliced onions
2 tbs. olive oil
salt and pepper to taste
3 large tomatoes, seeded and
  chopped

2 tbs. tomato paste
1 tsp. dried oregano
½ tsp. dried basil
½ tsp. salt
¼ tsp. pepper
12 oz. grated cheese

Sauté zucchini, mushrooms and onions in olive oil until soft but firm and set aside. Season with salt and pepper to taste. Mix tomatoes, tomato paste, oregano, basil, salt and pepper together. Spread mixture on pizza dough. Add grated cheese and sautéed vegetables. Bake on a low rack in a 450° oven for about 25 minutes.

NOTE: For a puffier crust, let dough rise in its shaped form for 30 minutes before adding the topping.

ZUCCHINI LASAGNA

Servings: 8

Here's a "pseudo" lasagna made with vegetables and cheese but no pasta!

2 lb. rehydrated zucchini slices
2 cups ricotta cheese
2 cups rehydrated tomato slices
1 cup rehydrated chopped onions
½ cup flour
1 tsp. salt
1 tsp. dried thyme
1 tsp. dried basil
1 cup Parmesan cheese
2 cups grated mozzarella or Jack cheese

Oil a casserole dish and place ½ of the rehydrated zucchini slices in bottom of dish. Top with half of the ricotta and tomato slices. On top, sprinkle on top half of the onions, flour, seasonings and cheeses. Repeat the whole process again using remaining ingredients. Bake in a 350° oven for 40 minutes or until heated through.

CHOCOLATE ZUCCHINI CAKE

Servings: 12

Zucchini grows in abundance, especially here in the Pacific Northwest. Zucchini gives a cake moisture and adds a nutritious ingredient.

3 eggs
1½ cups sugar
1½ tsp. vanilla
½ cup vegetable oil
2 cups flour
⅓ cup cocoa powder
1 tsp. baking soda

1½ tsp. baking powder
1 tsp. cinnamon
¼ tsp. salt
¾ cup buttermilk
2 cups rehydrated shredded zucchini
1½ cups chopped nuts
¾ cups dehydrated grapes (raisins)

Heat oven to 350°. Grease and flour a tube pan. Using a mixer, beat eggs, add sugar and vanilla and beat well. Beat in oil until well blended. Mix together flour, cocoa powder, baking soda, baking powder, cinnamon and salt. Add to egg mixture along with buttermilk. Stir in zucchini, nuts and dehydrated grapes (raisins). Pour into prepared pan and bake 50 minutes or until a knife inserted in center comes out clean. Cool 10 minutes and invert onto a plate. Cool and frost with chocolate icing or sprinkle with powdered sugar.

MEAT JERKY

Beef jerky is the most popular dried meat. But don't limit yourself just to beef. The same technique and most marinades work well for game meats and poultry.

TECHNIQUE:

1. Use lean meat (if using beef, I like flank steak or top round steak) and cut off any visible fat. (Fat can make dried meats turn rancid with time.)

2. Cut the meat (the standard way is with the grain, but I have found that it is more tender when cutting slices against the grain) into long narrow strips about ¼-inch thick. It is easier to cut meat into thin slices if you partially freeze the meat ahead of time. Meat should be cut before drying because fresh meat is a lot easier to cut than dried meat.

3. If choosing to marinate, place meat in marinade of your choice for at least 1 hour and up to 24 hours in the refrigerator; drain.

4. Dry in a single layer at 145° for approximately 5 to 10 hours (usually about 6 hours) or until meat is pliable but does not break when bent.

Occasionally check meat and remove any excess oils from the surface of the meat with a paper towel. If choosing to use larger cuts of meat, drying time will increase considerably.

5. Cool the meat thoroughly and store in airtight containers. I prefer to store dried meats in the freezer unless I plan to use them immediately. (This guarantees freshness, less chance of rancidity from the fat in meat and if the meat wasn't dried properly, less chance of food poisoning).

6. For estimating the amount of meat you will need, remember meat will dry to about ¼ of its fresh weight.

GROUND MEAT JERKY

- Use lean or extra-lean ground meat.
- Mix with spices, sauces, flavorings, etc. There are jerky spice mixes available from the commercial dehydrator companies.
- If you have a jerky press, follow instructions in booklet. If not:

1. Mix the meat with spices.
2. Roll the meat to about ⅛-inch thick between 2 pieces of waxed paper.

3. Place the meat on plastic wrap on solid plastic trays used to make leathers.
4. Dry for about 1 to 2 hours or until meat can be handled without falling apart.
5. Remove the meat from the trays and the plastic wrap.
6. With a paper towel, blot off any excess fat on the surface of the meat.
7. With scissors, cut into strips and return to your regular drying trays.
8. Continue drying until meat is pliable. Check periodically for excess fat and blot with paper towels.
9. Store in air-tight containers in the freezer.

DRIED COOKED MEATS
1. Cook the meat and trim off any excess fat.
2. Cut into ½-inch cubes.
3. Dry at 145° for approximately 6 to 12 hours or until meat appears hard and crisp with no signs of moisture.

NOTE: Sometimes the meat is a little more tender if you reduce the temperature to about 125° towards the end of the drying time.

4. Store in an air-tight container and freeze.
5. To rehydrate: Soak the meat in boiling water or broth until it plumps, approximately 45 minutes to 1 hour. Then simmer for 20 minutes.

USES FOR DRIED MEATS

- Raw or cooked meats can be dried and reconstituted to use in hot dishes like casseroles, stews, soups, etc.

- For all kinds of outdoor sports (hiking, camping, canoeing, fishing, horseback riding) dried meat can be a quick snack by itself or mixed with dried vegetables and rehydrated into soups, stews, etc.

- By reconstituting finely chopped or powdered dried meats with buttermilk or mayonnaise (and a little water, if necessary), you can produce the base for sandwich spreads. Add seasoning of your choice and chopped pickles if desired.

- Finely chopped dried meats or powdered meat can be rehydrated with water, chicken stock or milk to be used for baby food or "soft" food for older people.

- Indians used to make pemmican for survival on the trail and to make it through rough winters. It was an powdered mixture that usually contained dried meat, fat and dried berries. Some mixed in dried corn, other dried vegetables and sometimes grains. If you are an avid outdoors person and want to experiment, I would suggest adding spices and herbs to the mixture for a more palatable meal.

MARINADES FOR MEATS

STANDARD JERKY MARINADE

½ cup soy sauce
½ cup Worcestershire sauce
2 tbs. catsup
1¼ tsp. salt
½ tsp. pepper

2 tbs. brown sugar or white sugar
1 garlic clove, well-mashed
½ tsp. onion powder
2 lbs. lean meat cut into strips

Mix all ingredients together and marinate meat strips for at least 1 hour before drying.

SWEET AND SOUR JERKY MARINADE

½ cup red wine vinegar (I prefer
  balsamic)
1 tsp. garlic powder
2 tsp. salt
¾ cup pineapple juice

½ cup brown sugar
¼ cup soy sauce
¼ tsp. ground ginger
3 lbs. lean meat cut into strips

Mix all ingredients together. Place meat strips in marinade and refrigerate for at least 6 hours. Stir mixture occasionally to make sure all meat is covered. Dry following the technique on page 154.

HOT JERKY MARINADE

2 tsp. chili powder
2 tsp. dried garlic powder
2 tsp. dried onion powder
2 tsp. pepper
2 tbs. salt
1 tsp. brown sugar
½ tsp. cayenne
½ to 1 tsp. liquid smoke
1 cup water
2 lbs. lean meat cut into strips

Mix all ingredients together and pour over meat strips. Refrigerate for at least 6 hours and dry according to technique on page 154.

SPICY JERKY MARINADE

6 tbs. vegetable oil
1 cup soy sauce
6 tbs. brown sugar
3 tbs. sherry
2 tsp. finely minced garlic
¾ tsp. ground ginger
few dashes of Tabasco, optional
3 lbs. lean meat

Mix all ingredients together and marinate meat for at least 6 hours in the refrigerator. Dry using the technique on page 154.

SPECIAL NOTE: I tried an assortment of bottled marinades, teriyaki sauces, barbecue sauces and even dressings and everyone loved the new flavors. So if time is limited, consider simply using bottled sauces as a good alternative.

SPICED GROUND MEAT JERKY

3 lbs. lean ground meat
2 tbs. Worcestershire sauce
1 tsp. dried onion powder
1 tsp. brown sugar
¾ tsp. pepper
1 tbs. tomato paste

Mix all ingredients together. Fry a small amount of mixture and taste. Adjust seasonings to your personal preference. Then dry using the technique on page 154.

ITALIAN GROUND MEAT JERKY

4 lbs. lean ground meat
3 cups grated Parmesan cheese
1 tsp. dried oregano
2 tsp. dried parsley
2 tsp. seasoning salt
½ tsp. basil
2 tsp. garlic powder

Mix all ingredients together. Fry a small amount of mixture and taste. Adjust seasonings to your personal preference. Dry using the technique on page 154.

FISH JERKY

Fish jerky is not as popular as meat jerky because of the high salt content. The fish must be soaked in a salt brine before drying. Salt brine solution consists of 1 cup salt to 2 quarts cold water.

1. Use only very fresh and lean fish. The high-oil fishes such as salmon or smelt do not dry as well.

2. Cut fish fillets into ¼-inch strips and soak in salt brine for 30 minutes. Remove and rinse with cold water.

3. Liberally sprinkle both sides of rinsed fish with a dry cure seasoning (about 1 tablespoon per 2 pounds of fish).

4. Place fish in an airtight container and refrigerate for about 6 hours.

5. Place seasoned fish on drying trays in a single layer. Dry at 145° for approximately 12 to 14 hours or until firm, dry and tough but not crumbly).

6. Cool completely and store in airtight containers in the freezer.

FISH DRY CURE RECIPES

STANDARD DRY CURE

2 tbs. salt
2 tsp. dried onion powder
1 tsp. dried garlic powder
1 tbs. liquid smoke, or to taste

¼ cup soy sauce
dash Tabasco sauce
4 lbs. lean fish strips

Mix salt, onion powder and garlic powder together. In a separate bowl, mix liquid smoke, soy sauce and Tabasco together. Spread liquid mixture over fish and sprinkle with salt mixture. Refrigerate for about 6 hours and dry using the technique on page 161.

HERB-FLAVORED DRY CURE

2 tbs. salt
1 tsp. dried celery flakes
4 tbs. dried parsley flakes
½ tsp. crushed dried bay leaf
1 tsp. pepper

¼ tsp. thyme
2 tsp. onion powder
¼ cup white wine
4 lbs. lean fish strips

Mix all dry ingredients together. Rub fish strips with white wine and sprinkle with herb mixture. Refrigerate for about 6 hours and dry according to the technique on page 161.

BABY FOODS

VEGETABLE POWDER

Using vegetables that are very dry and brittle, simply chop into small pieces and mix in a blender until powdery. Store in air-tight glass jars in a dark, cool area.

VEGETABLES
Makes: 1 cup

1 cup hot water or milk ⅓ cup powdered dried vegetables

Pour hot water or milk over vegetable powder and rehydrate for approximately 20 minutes. Then pour into a blender and mix until smooth.

NOTE: If using milk for your rehydrating liquid, consider using goat milk because it is the least allergenic of the milks available and the least mucous-forming.

MEAT AND VEGETABLE COMBINATION
Makes: 1½ cups

1 cup hot water or milk 3 tbs. chopped cooked meat
⅓ cup powdered dried vegetables

Pour hot water or milk over the vegetable powder and rehydrate for approximately 20 minutes. Add chopped cooked meat and puree until smooth in a blender.

FRUIT PUREE

Makes: 1 cup

½ cup dried fruit or dried fruit leathers

½ to 1 cup hot water

Chop dried fruit into small pieces. Pour hot water over fruit (quantity of water depends on the fruit used and how thick or thin you like it) and rehydrate for approximately 30 minutes. Puree in a blender until smooth. Strain if desired.

Optional: Add fruit puree to 1 cup baby cereal for a sweetened cereal your baby will love.

FRUIT PUDDING

Makes: 2 cups

½ cup chopped dried fruit of choice
1 cup boiling water
2 egg yolks
¾ cup milk

1 tbs. cornstarch
sweeteners to taste (honey, fruit juice concentrate, sugar, etc.)

Pour boiling water over dried fruit and rehydrate about 20 minutes. Puree until smooth in a blender. Add egg yolks and milk and continue to blend until smooth. Add cornstarch and sweetener to taste; blend. Cook over medium heat, in a saucepan, until thickened. Remove from heat, cool and chill.

CANNED FOOD

I have tried many different kinds of canned products and have been very pleased with the results. Tomato sauces, ragu, canned stews, canned baked beans, your favorite chili recipe and even thick soups can be dehydrated to make quick, lightweight "hikers'" food.

1. Simply pour the canned product or your own cooled recipe onto a solid plastic tray or plastic wrap.

2. Dry at 145° for approximately 10 hours or until brittle. Sauces can be dried like fruit leathers: when pliable, roll and store using the same technique.

3. Cool and store in airtight jars in the freezer.

4. To rehydrate: Add a small amount of boiling water at a time, and check every 10 minutes to see if it can absorb additional hot water (this will prevent the flavor from becoming too diluted).

CROUTONS

Croutons are very easy to make and a great way to use leftover bread before it turns moldy.

1. Depending on the use of the crumbs, cut up into ½-inch squares (with or without crusts). Crusts are usually removed when crumbs are used for coating in frying. Save the crusts, dry and use as topping on casseroles to absorb oils.

2. For plain croutons or crumbs, simply lay out on trays and dry at 145° for approximately 2 to 3 hours or until crisp. For crumbs, place dried croutons in a blender or food processor and pulverize into fine crumbs.

3. For seasoned croutons, mix together 1 tsp. salt (or salt-free seasoning blend), 1 tsp. paprika and 3 tbs. finely ground Parmesan cheese in a brown paper bag. Toss dried croutons with a little melted butter. While hot, drop into the bag with the seasoning and shake bag to coat the croutons.

NOTE: Another alternative is to substitute dried or fresh herbs in place of the cheese.

DRIED FLOWERS

Many flowers can be dried in the dehydrator. You will have to experiment a little and keep the temperature very low. To add fragrance to potpourri, use "essential oils" or fragrant oils found in craft shops and health food stores.

1. The flowers should be dry to start with, best if picked after the dew has dried and before the night damp sets in. Dry the flowers as soon as possible after picking.

2. The best condition for drying flowers is a dry, warm, dark, clean and well-ventilated area, which makes a dehydrator an ideal setting. Flowers will retain the best color and condition when dried quickly.

3. A low temperature should be used to retain the natural oils.

4. Strip off the leaves or if you prefer to keep the foliage, discard brown or damaged leaves.

5. Place on the drying trays in a single layer, avoiding any overlapping.

6. Drying times will vary considerably depending on the size of the flower and the amount of foliage. Dry at 100° generally from 6 to 72 hours.

HERB POTPOURRI

6 cups rose petals
1 cup dried thyme
1 cup dried rosemary
1 cup dried sweet marjoram
1 cup dried lavendar
1 cup dried sweet basil

6 crushed bay leaves
1 tbs. allspice
2 tbs. dried lemon peel
2 tbs. dried orange peel
1 tsp. anise seed

Mix all ingredients together and store in an airtight jar in a cool, dark area. When ready to use, simply pour into a pretty dish and strategically place around the house.

MINT POTPOURRI

2 cups dried lavendar
1 cup dried mint leaves, left whole
½ cup dried thyme
¼ cup dried rosemary
few drops of essential oils of your
  choice

few dried geranium petals
few dried blue bachelor's buttons
few dried flower petals of choice
  (dephinium, rose, etc.)

Mix together and store in an airtight container. Keep in a dark, cool area until ready to use.

HERBS

The leaves of most herbs should be green and tender and harvested just before the plant begins to flower.

1. Rinse leaves and stems with cold water and shake off excess water. Pat dry with towels and cut off dead, mushy, or discolored leaves before drying.

2. For herb seeds, pick when the pods have changed color but before they begin to shatter. Spread the pods on the drying trays, dry and rub the pods between your palms to release the seeds.

3. Always dry herbs at a low temperature because high temperatures destroy natural oils.

4. Spread herbs (stems and leaves) loosely on a tray and dry at 95° to 100° for approximately 3 to 5 hours. Herbs with larger leaves like cilantro will take longer.

5. It is best to dry herbs separately other foods because the produce will create a more moist environment which increases drying time.

6. Dry herbs on stems. When completely dry and brittle, strip leaves off stems.

7. Do not grind the leaves into a powder before storing. It is best to grind into a powder with a mortar and pestle or crushed in your hands just before using.

8. Store in tightly-closed containers in a cool, dark place. Do not store in paper bags, because the natural oils will be absorbed by the paper, which reduces the potency of the herb.

- Dried herbs have 3 to 4 times the potency of fresh herbs.

- Eight ounces of fresh herbs will yield about 1 ounce dried.

- Dried herbs and spices should keep well for 6 months to 1 year.

HERB TEA COMBINATIONS
- spearmint, camomile and blueberry

- dried orange peel and blackberry leaves

- rose hips, orange peel and gingeroot

- spearmint, peppermint and lemon peel

- camomile, hops and valerian (good as a sedative)

LEATHERS

FRUIT LEATHERS

1. Choose fresh, ripe fruit. Wash, remove stems, peel, cut out any bruised sections and puree in a blender until very smooth. Puree should be pouring consistency. If making berry puree, consider straining out the seeds before drying.

NOTE: Canned fruit can be used. Simply drain and puree (sometimes the addition of a little lemon juice freshens the flavor).

2. Taste puree. If fruit needs sweetening, add 1 tbs. honey, fruit juice concentrate or white corn syrup per quart of puree, taste again and repeat procedure until appropriate sweetness is obtained. If desired, add spices or flavored extracts for additional flavor. Continue with step 3.

NOTE: Do not sweeten with sugar. It tends to crystallize, causing a granular texture.

VEGETABLE LEATHERS

1. Wash vegetables, peel (when appropriate), steam blanch, chop into pieces, and puree in a blender until smooth. If needed, add enough water to make it blend easily. Combining several varieties of vegetables together

usually produces a better flavor.

2. Add spices or herbs to your personal taste before drying. Certain vegetables like tomatoes (which is actually a fruit, used like a vegetable) may have a tendency towards bitterness. To reduce this, add a little sweetener to taste. Continue with step 3.

FOR FRUIT *AND* VEGETABLE LEATHERS

3. Spread fruit or vegetable puree approximately ¼-inch thick onto solid plastic trays or onto heavy plastic wrap stretched over your regular drying trays. Leave a 1-inch border around the edges to allow for spreading during the drying procedure.

4. If desired, sprinkle leathers before drying with chopped nuts, coconut, chopped dates, cereals, granola, raisins, sesame seeds, sunflower seeds, etc. to add texture.

5. Dry at 100° for approximately 18 hours or until pliable and leather-like. Times may vary according to type of produce used and thickness of the puree.

6. Remove from the dryer and while still warm, roll. Wrap plastic wrap around the outside of the roll and store in an airtight container. I prefer to store vegetable leathers and fruit leathers covered with nuts in the refrigerator or freezer.

- Leathers can be unrolled, filled and rerolled for a great appetizer or dessert. Cut the filled leathers into 1-inch rounds. (Possible fillings: cream cheese, chocolate, jams, nut butters, cheese and thick fruit fillings).

TROUBLE-SHOOTING FRUIT LEATHER PROBLEMS

- Leather sticks to surface: Coat the solid tray or plastic wrap with vegetable spray or a small amount of oil before pouring on the puree. Do not use foil or waxed paper. Sometimes berries have too much pectin. Mix with other fruit to reduce the pectin content.

- Uneven drying: Tilt and shake drying trays until puree is evenly distributed. Sometimes it may be due to the uneven distribution of heat in the dryer. Rotate the shelves.

- Brittle leathers: This problem can be caused by overdrying or too high heat, causing leather to dry too quickly.

- Dark leathers: Add ascorbic acid to the puree to help prevent darkening. Sometimes cooking the fruit ahead of time helps, but I prefer not to do this since it destroys nutrition and can reduce flavor. Also, air and light exposure during storage can cause darker leathers.

- Molding: Leathers are not dried sufficiently before storing or are exposed to moisture during storage.

- Puree too thin: Combine with thicker purees or cook to reduce water content.

- Puree too thick: Add fruit juices or water to the puree or combine with thinner purees.

POSSIBLE FRUIT LEATHER COMBINATIONS

Use fruit juice concentrate, honey or white corn syrup for sweeteners; use enough for your own taste.

- 6 cups chopped apple and ½ cup chopped dried grapes (raisins)

- 5 cups chopped apple, 1 cup cooked rhubarb, sweetener

- 3 cups chopped apple, 3 cups berries, sweetener

- 5 cups chopped apricot, 1 cup mashed banana, vanilla to taste

- 4 cups mashed banana, 2 cups chopped pineapple, sweetener

- 3 cups chopped apricot, 3 cups chopped plums, sweetener
- 4 cups chopped strawberries, 2 cups cooked rhubarb, sweetener
- 4 cups mashed bananas, 2 cups crunchy peanut butter, sweetener
- 3 cups cranberries, 3 cups chopped apples, sweetener
- 3 cups chopped peaches, 3 cups chopped pears, 1 tsp. cinnamon, sweetener
- 4 cups cherries, 2 cups chopped apples, 1 tsp. lemon juice, sweetener
- 2 cups grapes and 4 cups chopped apples

NUTS

1. Shell nuts and rinse with hot water. (I have found that this will remove dust, as well as a residual oil that seems to cause allergic reactions in some people).

2. Spread nuts onto trays in a single layer.

3. Dry at 90° to 100° for approximately 24 to 48 hours or until brittle. If choosing to use nuts with the shells, drying time will be about 10 hours. To test, open a shelled nut. The nutmeat should be tender but not shriveled.

4. Allow nuts to cool. Store in glass jars or plastic bags. Because nuts contain so much oil, there is a tendency for the oils to become rancid, so I choose to freeze nuts to guarantee freshness.

5. When ready to use the nuts, allow the jar to come to room temperature first. The frozen nuts will immediately draw moisture from the environment which leads to possible molding or faster rancidity.

NUT AND FRUIT MIX

Makes: 10 cups

This is only one combination of fruit and nuts. You can really be creative with all the endless possible mixtures of this high protein energy food.

1 lb. toasted almonds
1 lb. toasted Brazil nuts
1 lb. toasted cashew nuts
½ lb. toasted pine nuts
½ lb. mixed dried grapes (raisins)
¼ cup Marsala, sweet vermouth or fruit juice
¼ cup shredded coconut
¼ cup salted sunflower seeds
¼ cup chopped dried fruit (apricot, pears, apples, etc.)
salt and/or Worcestershire sauce to taste, optional

Mix nuts together and set aside. In a saucepan, mix dried grapes (raisins) and wine (or fruit juice) together and bring to a boil. Immediately reduce heat and simmer until liquid has evaporated, about 20 minutes, remove from heat and cool. Combine mixture with remaining ingredients and mix well. If desired, add salt and/or Worcestershire sauce to taste.

GRANOLA

Makes: 10 to 12 cups

This is a great recipe that can have almost any dried fruit added to it.

4 cups old-fashioned oats
1 cup sunflower seeds
½ cup sesame seeds
1 cup coconut
¾ cup wheat germ
½ cup bran flakes
½ cup soy grits, optional
1½ cups cashews or peanuts

¼ cup non-instant powdered milk
¾ cup vegetable oil
½ cup brown sugar
¾ cup honey
1 tsp. vanilla
1 to 2 cups chopped dried fruits, your choice

Preheat oven to 275°. Grease a large baking pan or sided cookie sheet. Mix oats, sunflower seeds, sesame seeds, coconut, wheat germ, bran flakes, soy grits (added for protein) and powdered milk together and set aside. Mix oil, brown sugar, honey and vanilla together and toss with oat mixture. Bake for approximately 1 hour, stirring every 15 minutes, until mixture turns golden brown. Remove from oven, add chopped dried fruits, and spread out on wax paper to let cool. Crumble with your hands to separate.

GRANOLA BARS

Simply bake the granola about 15 minutes less. Remove from the oven (do not add dried fruits to granola bars) and press warm granola onto a well-greased shallow baking pan (add a little peanut butter if desired). Bake at 350° for 15 to 20 minutes, remove from oven and cut into bars.

YOGURT

1 quart milk (fat content according
  to personal preference)
½ cup powdered milk
2 to 3 tbs. plain commercial yogurt
  (or 1 tbs. yogurt starter)

flavored extracts to taste, optional
dried chopped fruits to taste, optional
sweetener to taste (honey, fruit juice
  concentrates, corn syrup), optional

In a saucepan, mix milk and powdered milk together and hear to scalding, remove from heat and let cool to 110°. If using plain commercial yogurt, simply mix well with cooled scalded milk. If using yogurt starter, add yogurt starter to ⅓ cup scalded milk and mix well. Return mixture to remaining milk.

Put a thermometer in your dehydrator and adjust the controls until you get 108°. Pour into flat containers and cover. Place in dehydrator for 2 to 4 hours at 108° or longer if temperature is too low. After yogurt is made, cool. If desired, stir in flavored extracts, dried fruits and/or sweeteners to personal taste.

NOTE: Getting the temperature exact is *very crucial*. If the temperature is too high, the yogurt will curdle and if the temperature is too low, the yogurt will take considerably longer to thicken.

YOGURT SNACK DROPS
flavored yogurt
toasted chopped nuts or chopped dried fruit, optional

Drop ½ tsp. of flavored yogurt on oiled solid sheets or plastic wrap. If desired, sprinkle drops with chopped toasted nuts or chopped dried fruit. Dry at 135° for approximately 10 hours or until chewy. Remove drops from the sheet while warm. Chill and store in the refrigerator or freezer.

YOGURT ROLLS
flavored yogurt
chopped toasted nuts, coconut, chopped dried fruit, optional

Spread about 2 cups of flavored yogurt on oiled solid sheet or plastic wrap about ⅛-inch thick. If desired, sprinkle with optional ingredients. Dry at 125° for approximately 10 hours or until leathery. Remove from sheet while warm and roll. Store in refrigerator or freezer.

INDEX

SERVE CREATIVE, EASY, NUTRITIOUS MEALS WITH NITTY GRITTY® COOKBOOKS

The Versatile Rice Cooker
The Dehydrator Cookbook
Waffles
The Coffee Book
The Bread Machine Cookbook
The Bread Machine Cookbook II
The Bread Machine Cookbook III
The Bread Machine Cookbook IV
The Sandwich Maker Cookbook
The Juicer Book
The Juicer Book II
Bread Baking (traditional), revised
The Kid's Cookbook, revised
The Kid's Microwave Cookbook
15-Minute Meals for 1 or 2
Recipes for the 9x13 Pan

Extra-Special Crockery Pot Recipes
Chocolate Cherry Tortes and Other Lowfat Delights
Lowfat American Favorites
Lowfat International Cuisine
The Hunk Cookbook
Now That's Italian!
Fabulous Fiber Cookery
Low Salt, Low Sugar, Low Fat Desserts
What's for Breakfast?
Healthy Cooking on the Run
Healthy Snacks for Kids
Creative Soups & Salads
Quick & Easy Pasta Recipes, revised

Muffins, Nut Breads and More
The Barbecue Book
The Wok
New Ways with Your Wok
Quiche & Soufflé Cookbook
Cooking for 1 or 2
Meals in Minutes
New Ways to Enjoy Chicken
Favorite Seafood Recipes
No Salt, No Sugar, No Fat Cookbook
New International Fondue Cookbook
Favorite Cookie Recipes
Authentic Mexican Cooking
Fisherman's Wharf Cookbook
The Creative Lunch Box

Write or call for our free catalog.
Bristol Publishing Enterprises, Inc.
P.O. Box 1737, San Leandro, CA 94577
(800)346-4889; in California (510)895-4461